Adobe
Photoshop™

Library of Congress Catalog No.: 93-73013

ISBN: 1-56830-054-9

10 9 8 7 6 5 4 3 2   First Printing: October 1993

Printed in the United States of America by Shepard Poorman Communications, Indianapolis, Indiana.

Published simultaneously in Canada.

Adobe Press books are published and distributed by Hayden Books, a division of Prentice Hall Computer Publishing. For individual orders, or for educational, corporate, or retail sales accounts, call 1-800-428-5331. For information address Hayden Books, 201 West 103rd Street, Indianapolis, IN 46290.

CONTENTS

GETTING STARTED

Adobe Photoshop™ is an image-editing program that lets you create and produce high-quality digital images, without the expense of high-end workstations. As an electronic darkroom, Adobe Photoshop lets you manipulate scanned photolithographs, slides, and original artwork in a variety of ways. The program combines a full range of selection tools, painting and editing tools, color-correction tools, and special effect capabilities (such as rotation and filtering) that allow you to edit images in one of several color modes, including RGB and CMYK. As a production tool, Adobe Photoshop produces high-quality color separations and halftones that you can print using the numerous printing options.

PREREQUISITES

Before beginning to use Adobe Photoshop, you should have a working knowledge of Microsoft® Windows™ and its operating conventions. You should know how to use the mouse and standard Windows menus and commands. You should also know how to open, save, and close files. If you need to review these techniques, see the documentation that comes with your personal computer.

ABOUT *CLASSROOM IN A BOOK*™

Classroom in a Book teaches you the basics (as well as some advanced techniques) for using Adobe Photoshop's features and capabilities. When you've completed this hands-on educational book, you will have a good working knowledge of the program and will be well on your way to becoming an experienced Adobe Photoshop user.

Classroom in a Book is created by Adobe Systems Educational Services group. The lesson topics for this book are based on tasks users and students in test-teaching classes found most challenging to learn. The *Classroom in a Book* team, based on the feedback of users, has created this hands-on educational book.

This hands-on educational book includes 13 lessons. Each lesson contains step-by-step instructions to help you complete a specific design project.

In these lessons, you will learn how to do the following:

- make and manipulate selections

- use the painting and editing tools

- create and use masks

- store saved selections in channels

- color-correct all or part of an image

- resize and change the resolution of an image

- convert from one image type to another

- prepare color separations

- print images

- use Adobe Photoshop with Adobe Illustrator™ artwork

Lessons 3, 6, 9, and 13 are review lessons that give you a chance to practice the skills you've learned in the previous lessons.

Classroom in a Book is not meant to replace documentation that comes with Adobe Photoshop. Only the commands and options used in the lessons are explained in this book. For comprehensive information about all of the program's features, refer to the *Adobe Photoshop User Guide*. You will find the *Quick Reference Card* packaged with Adobe Photoshop a useful companion as you work through the lessons in this book. For additional practice in using Adobe Photoshop, try doing the lessons in the *Adobe Photoshop Tutorial*. For instructions on advanced techniques, see *Beyond the Basics*.

SYSTEM REQUIREMENTS

To use Adobe Photoshop, you need:

• An Intel® 80386- or 80486-based or faster PC with at least 4 megabytes (MB) of application random-access memory (RAM) dedicated to the Adobe Photoshop application

• MS-DOS 5.0 or greater and Microsoft Windows 3.1 or greater

• A color Standard VGA display adapter and compatible monitor

• A mouse or other compatible pointing device

• Current Windows drivers

SYSTEM RECOMMENDATIONS

In addition, Adobe Systems recommends the following hardware and software:

• An Intel 80486 or Pentium processor or a faster processor

• 8 MB or more of application RAM dedicated to the Adobe Photoshop application

• Super VGA using 256 colors or millions of colors at a resolution of 800 x 600 or 1024 x 768

• A 24-bit color display adapter and compatible color monitor

• A PC-compatible scanner

• A PostScript™ printer

• Acceleration products bearing the *Adobe charged* logo

INSTALLING ADOBE PHOTOSHOP

Before you begin using Adobe Photoshop, make a backup copy of the program disks to work with during installation. For instructions on how to copy disks, refer to your Windows user documentation.

If you already have Adobe Photoshop installed on your computer, please skip the next few installation sections and proceed to "Installing the Classroom in a Book CD-ROM directories" on page 4.

You begin by installing the Adobe Type Manager™ (ATM™) program contained on the program disks. You then install the Adobe Photoshop program.

Installing the ATM software

The Adobe Photoshop package includes Adobe Type Manager, which allows you to take advantage of the Type 1 typefaces when creating text in a document. ATM is font software that generates sharp, clear characters of any size on your computer screen and on non-PostScript printers.

The ATM installer installs the ATM software and Type 1 fonts on your hard disk. For each font you want to use, you install the outline fonts and one bitmapped font. ATM automatically creates bitmapped characters of any size for the font.

The ATM software requires about 500K of disk space, and each Type 1 font requires about 40K of disk space. The 13 standard Type 1 fonts included with ATM require at least 1.2 MB of disk space.

To install the ATM software on your system:

1 Quit all Windows applications.

2 Start Windows 3.1 or higher. The Windows desktop appears.

3 Insert the ATM program disk into drive a: or b:.

4 From the Program Manager, choose Run from the File menu.

5 Type a:\install (where a: is the drive indicator) and click OK. The ATM Installer dialog box appears.

If ATM is already running, a dialog box appears informing you that a version of ATM is running. Click OK, then click OK again to replace the old version of ATM with the new version. The Installer turns off the currently running version of ATM and restarts Windows.

6 Specify directories for the Type 1 font outline files and font metrics files. You can accept the defaults or change them.

The default directory for the font outline (PFB) files is C:PSFONTS. The default directory for the font metrics (PFM) files is C:\PSFONTS\PFM.

If you change the target directory for PostScript outline fonts, the target directory for font metrics files is automatically updated to the same path, and a PFM subdirectory is added. You can accept this name or enter a new directory name.

7 Click Install. A status window displays the progress of the installation.

When the installation is complete and all files have been copied to your hard disk, the final installation screen appears stating that installation was successful and prompting you to restart Windows. You must restart Windows to use the ATM program.

8 Click Restart Windows. The program restarts windows, turns on the ATM program, and makes the Type 1 fonts available in your application Fonts menus.

If you have upgraded from an earlier version of ATM, both the new program icon and the old program icon may appear in the Main program group. Delete the old program icon by selecting it and choosing Delete from the File menu. When you upgrade ATM, the Control Panel settings (such as font cache size and installed fonts) are preserved.

Installing Adobe Photoshop

Use the following procedure to install the Adobe Photoshop program files.

To install the Adobe Photoshop program:

1 Start Windows, if you have not already done so.

2 Insert the Adobe Photoshop Disk 1 into drive a: or b:.

3 From the Program Manager, choose Run from the File menu.

Note: If you are using a desktop manager other than Program Manager, first run the Program Manager application PROGMAN.EXE, and then follow step 3. Running the installer from other than the Program Manager may produce unexpected results.

4 Type a: pssetup.exe (where a: is the drive indicator) and click OK. The Adobe Photoshop Installer dialog box appears, displaying the amount of disk space required to install all program files and the amount of disk space available.

5 Deselect any file groups that you do not want to install.

6 Be sure to install the Plug-ins files. If you do not install these files, many of the Adobe Photoshop file formats and Adobe Photoshop filters will not be available.

7 Accept the default target drive and directory, or type a new drive and directory.

8 Click Install. Click OK at the request to complete the registration card.

9 Enter your name, organization, and serial number of the program.

10 Click OK. The Installer dialog box appears.

11 Click OK to begin the installation.

12 Follow the on-screen instructions, inserting additional disks and clicking OK as prompted.

4

When installation is complete, a message appears indicating that the installation was successful.

13 Click OK to return to the Program Manager.

For more information on the Adobe Photoshop application installation, see the Getting Started document with your documentation.

INSTALLING THE *CLASSROOM IN A BOOK* CD-ROM DIRECTORIES

The *Classroom in a Book* CD-ROM disc includes directories containing all the electronic files for the *Classroom in a Book* lessons. Each lesson has its own directory. You will need to install these directories on your hard disk to access the files for the lessons. To save room, you can install the directories for each lesson as you need them.

The files are locked for your protection, so that you don't inadvertently write over the original files. When you open the files, you will see an alert box telling you that you cannot save changes. Click OK to open the file, then give the file a new name when you save it.

To install the *Classroom in a Book* directories:

1 Start Windows, if it is not already running.

2 From the File Manager double-click the Photoshop group.

3 Choose Create Directory from the File menu. The Create Directory dialog box appears.

4 Type **PHSCIB** and click OK.

5 Copy the directories from the CD-ROM disk into this directory.

CREATING A PROJECTS DIRECTORY

While you're working through *Classroom in a Book,* you will create and save many Adobe Photoshop files. Before you begin working in Adobe Photoshop, create a new directory on your hard

disk and name it *Projects.* You can place this directory on the desktop or you can put it in the PHSCIB directory. When you save your first file, the Projects directory will be available from within Adobe Photoshop. Using a separate file to store your work should help you manage your files more efficiently.

STARTING ADOBE PHOTOSHOP FOR THE FIRST TIME

1 Be sure the PHSCIB directory is open.

2 Choose Create Directory from the File menu.

3 Type **Projects** and click OK.

The first time you start Adobe Photoshop you need to enter some personal information. You will probably want to do this before you begin the *Classroom in a Book* lessons.

To start Adobe Photoshop:

1 Start Windows, if it is not already running.

2 From the Program Manager, double-click the Adobe Photoshop program icon in the Adobe group.

The Adobe Photoshop window appears. You are ready to create or open a document and start working.

3 Close Adobe Photoshop for now.

IMPROVING PERFORMANCE

A program's *performance* is the amount of time that it takes an application to complete certain operations, such as opening a file, sending a file to a printer, or redrawing the screen after you edit an image. In part, performance is determined by the type of computer and amount of memory you're using. See the *Adobe Photoshop Users Guide* for information on changing the application memory size with Adobe Photoshop.

Using virtual memory

Adobe Photoshop has a virtual memory scheme designed to optimize the application's performance. *Virtual memory* is temporary disk space used for storing data and performing computations on files during a work session when RAM is insufficient, In Photoshop, three to five times the file size is recommended for the virtual memory disk, also called the scratch disk. For information about assigning scratch disks, see Chapter 1, "Basic Concepts," in the *Adobe Photoshop User Guide.*

Using Windows virtual memory

Windows also has its own virtual memory management scheme. Photoshop's virtual memory scheme swaps image data to a hard drive if there is not enough RAM to contain the data. Windows virtual memory swaps active application programs to a hard disk when there is not enough memory to hold them all simultaneously.

Adding Windows virtual memory will not increase the amount of RAM available for Photoshop, because Adobe Photoshop uses only installed RAM and its own virtual memory scheme to maximize performance. However, you should not limit or decrease your Windows and other Windows applications. Instead, you should keep as much hard disk space available as possible so that Photoshop can use it as needed.

Maximizing performance

The best way to improve performance when using Adobe Photoshop is to increase the amount of RAM installed on your systems. Without buying additional RAM, you can maximize the program's performance several ways. See the Getting Started document for detailed information.

Managing fonts

Organizing your fonts efficiently can help improve overall system performance. If you are using Adobe Type Manager and plan on using large display sizes, be sure to increase the size of the ATM font cache to at least 256K, if your system has 8 MB or less of RAM, and to at least 512K if your system has more than 8 MB of RAM.

WORKING EFFICIENTLY

A key to working efficiently in Adobe Photoshop is to minimize the size of your files. Smaller files make all operations faster. Creative use of Adobe Photoshop's features, such as channels, multiple windows, and command shortcuts, can also help you work faster and more effectively.

Minimizing file size

Some Adobe Photoshop files, because of resolution or image complexity, are large files. You can increase efficiency by working with temporary files that contain only sections of the larger file, or you can try out changes on smaller versions of a large file.

Creating low-resolution files

One way to save time and space is to create a 72-dpi version of your file. Be sure to give this copy a unique name when you create it so that you don't overwrite your original high-resolution image.

A low-resolution document is useful for making initial editing and color corrections. If you're adjusting color, save the settings using the Save buttons in the color-adjustment dialog boxes. Once you know what features and dialog box settings produce the results you want, open the original file and repeat the steps. Then use the Load button to apply saved settings to the original file.

Using the keypad

To utilize the keypad on your keyboard, be sure the Num Lock key is activated.

Using channels

Try to develop the habit of saving complex selections in channels until you have finished editing a file. You can then easily load the selections without wasting time in reselecting. If you have a lot of selections, use the Duplicate command in the Calculate submenu to copy selections to another file. By loading the channels as selections from this second file, you can keep the size of the file you're working on manageable.

Making complex selections in Grayscale mode can save processing time, since grayscale images are about one-third the size of RGB images. Save the selection in a channel and then use the Duplicate command to copy the selections into a new channel of your original image. If you increase the contrast of a grayscale image, it's easier to select shapes of different colors. When you're working with 1-bit images, it's even faster to save a complex selection as a path.

Some Photoshop filters, such as the Distort filter, work only in RAM and don't use virtual memory. If you're having problems applying a filter to a color image, try applying it to each color channel individually. This applies the filter to a considerably smaller file, since each RGB channel is equal to about a third of the entire file size. A CMYK channel is about one-fourth the size of the entire file.

Working in two windows

You can save time by using the New Window command to open a second window for a document. For example, you can work on a magnified version of an image in one window while viewing the entire image in a second window, or you can use two windows to view the results of color corrections in the composite color channel and in an individual channel of an image.

Using shortcuts

Learn to use the command shortcuts that appear to the right of commands in menus. These are especially useful for operations that you perform frequently, such as displaying a specific command's dialog box or adjusting color levels.

There are also some procedural shortcuts that can save you time, such as magnifying (double-click the hand tool to fit an image in the window; double-click the zoom tool to display an image at actual size) and filling a selection with color (use Alt-Delete to fill with the foreground color). For more information on shortcuts, see the *Adobe Photoshop Quick Reference Card.*

Using Macintosh files on the PC

You can use Adobe Photoshop files saved on the Macintosh in Windows if you follow these guidelines:

• When saving an Adobe Photoshop version 2.5 or greater file on the Macintosh for use in Windows Adobe Photoshop version 2.5 or greater, name the file according to DOS-naming conventions, followed by the .PSD extension. All file information will be preserved.

• When saving an Adobe Photoshop version 2.0 file on the Macintosh for use in Windows Adobe Photoshop version 2.5 or greater, open the 2.0 file in Macintosh version 2.5 or greater and save the file in the 2.5 or greater format using the correct DOS-naming conventions and .PSD extension. If you do not have Macintosh version 2.5 or greater, you can use Macintosh version 2.0 to save the file, specifying the PC TIFF file format. Any channels saved with the document will be lost, however, the file's resolution will be preserved. See the *Adobe Photoshop Getting Started* document for more information.

LE MONDE

B

Gourmet Visions

LESSON 1: MAKING SELECTIONS

Adobe Photoshop is a powerful image-editing program that allows you to edit and colorize images, retouch proofs, create original or composite artwork, and produce prepress color separations. Whether you're an art director, an electronic publisher, a photographer, an animator, a multimedia producer, or a service bureau, Adobe Photoshop gives you the tools you need to get top-quality, professional results.

Classroom in a Book teaches you the basics (as well as many of the advanced techniques) that you need to start getting the most out of Adobe Photoshop, right now. The projects in this book focus on a fictional international culinary corporation named Gourmet Visions. This mythical company contains several divisions that import and export foods and beverages, publish cookbooks, and manage a chain of specialty food markets. The projects you'll create in these lessons are those that might be produced by the Gourmet Visions art department.

Unlike a real work environment, *Classroom in a Book* is designed to let you move at your own pace, and even make mistakes! Although the lessons are designed with specific projects in mind, and provide step-by-step instructions to help you achieve these results, there is built-in room for exploration and experimentation. The goal of *Classroom in a Book* is not only to teach you Adobe Photoshop, but more importantly, to allow you to realize the power of your own imagination.

This lesson introduces you to Adobe Photoshop, and shows you how to make and work with selections in an Adobe Photoshop image. It should take you about 30 minutes to complete this lesson.

In this lesson, you'll learn how to do the following:

- calibrate your monitor

- open a file

- load a selection

- use the marquee and magic wand selection tools

- copy and paste a selection

- magnify and move around in an image

- add to and subtract from a selection

- zoom in and zoom out in an image

- save a selection

- choose and change the foreground color

- fill a selection

- save a file

At the end of this lesson you'll have an edited version of the beginning image, saved in a file that also contains a saved selection. This final image will serve as the starting point for the painting project in Lesson 2.

Source file (CRAB.PSD)   *Ending image (NEW CRAB.PSD)*

CALIBRATING YOUR SYSTEM

Before you begin working in Adobe Photoshop, you need to *calibrate* your monitor. Calibration is the process of adjusting your screen display and some Adobe Photoshop settings so that the colors you see when you display an Adobe Photoshop image match the colors you see in a final printed image.

All monitors display colors using a mixture of the primary *additive colors* of red, green, and blue (RGB). Combining these colors produces a large percentage of the visible spectrum. Your monitor can only display color using the RGB system.

When you print, the color you see is the result of color being absorbed or subtracted by the inks on the page. In theory, mixing the primary *subtractive colors* of cyan, magenta, and yellow (CMY) should produce black (K). In actuality, some extra black must be added to absorb all the color from a printed page.

You'll learn more about RGB and CMYK color in Lesson 7. For now, you just need to know that you calibrate your system to make the RGB colors you see on the screen match the CMYK colors used to print a final proof.

In this lesson, you'll calibrate your monitor and enter some values for printing inks and papers. Before you do your own work in Adobe Photoshop, you'll want to perform the entire calibration process as described in the *Adobe Photoshop User Guide*.

Standardizing your work environment

The first adjustment you'll make is to standardize your room lighting and monitor settings so that the calibration will be accurate for your work environment.

To adjust the lighting, brightness, and contrast:

1 Make sure your monitor has been on for about a half hour so that its display has stabilized.

2 Set the room lighting at the level you plan to maintain, then adjust the brightness and contrast controls on your monitor.

Because changes in lighting, brightness, and contrast can dramatically affect your display, try to keep the room free from external light sources. Tape down your brightness and contrast controls once you've set them.

3 Change the color of your screen to light gray to prevent background color from interfering with your color perception.

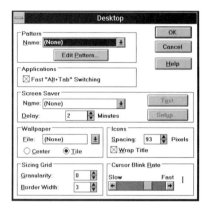

Calibrating your monitor

Calibrating your monitor consists of adjusting the monitor grays to make them as neutral as possible. This prevents your monitor from introducing a color cast to your images. You calibrate the monitor by first setting a target gamma, then adjusting the whites, the grays (gamma), the color balance, and finally the blacks.

Important: If you have a third-party monitor-calibration utility installed, use either that utility or the Adobe Photoshop Calibrate command. Using both utilities will miscalibrate the monitor. If you use a third-party calibration utility, you'll need to enter the values suggested by the utility into the Monitor Setup dialog box.

To calibrate your monitor:

1 Choose Preferences from the Edit menu and Monitor Setup from the submenu. Click Calibrate.

The Calibrate dialog box appears.

2 Click the White Pt button.

3 Hold up a piece of paper similar to the stock you'll be printing on and drag the three slider triangles until the monitor white matches that of the paper.

This adjustment compensates for the bluish tint found in most 13-inch monitor displays and the reddish tint found in most larger displays.

4 Drag the Gamma Adjustment slider until the gray areas in the gamma strip above the slider match the patterned gray areas in the strip (that is, the strip appears to be continuous-tone gray).

5 Click the Balance button, then drag the three slider triangles until the gray areas in the strip below the sliders become a neutral gray (that is, they contain no color tints).

This adjustment controls the monitor's mixture of red, green, and blue components and compensates for color casts in the monitor.

6 Click the Black Pt button, then drag the three slider triangles until there is no color tint in the shadow tones in the lower strip.

You may need to make further adjustments to your gamma setting after setting the white and black points.

7 Click OK to close the Calibrate dialog box.

Entering the Monitor Setup information

After adjusting the monitor, you enter the monitor settings in the Monitor Setup dialog box.

To enter the monitor settings:

1 If it's not already running, start Adobe Photoshop.

2 Choose Preferences from the File menu and Monitor Setup from the submenu. The Monitor Setup dialog box appears.

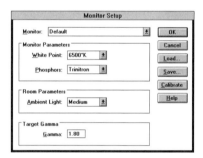

3 Choose your monitor from the Monitor pop-up menu.

4 Choose 6500K from the White Point pop-up menu for Monitor Parameters.

If you changed the monitor type, a different default White Point value might be displayed. Third-party calibration utilities sometimes require different temperature settings.

5 Choose Trinitron from the Phosphors pop-up menu (or the type for your particular monitor).

6 Choose High, Low, or Medium from the Ambient Light pop-up menu for Room Parameters.

A Medium setting indicates that the room lighting is about as bright as the image on the screen.

7 Enter 1.8 in the Gamma text box (or the gamma value suggested by your calibration utility) for Target Gamma.

8 Click OK to close the dialog box.

Entering the Printing Inks Setup information

Another important component in correct calibration is compensating for the printing inks and paper used to print the final image. Since printing inks have a specific density, ink types use varying amounts of coverage to produce the same colors. Similarly, certain papers absorb more or less of the printing ink to produce identical colors. You can think of the information you enter in the Printing Inks Setup dialog box as telling Adobe Photoshop what printed cyan looks like, what printed magenta looks like, and so on, given a certain set of inks and paper stock.

By adjusting the settings in the Printing Inks Setup dialog box, you can anticipate these ink and paper inconsistencies and allow for them in the monitor display. If you set these parameters before you begin working, you'll avoid unexpected surprises when you print your images.

To enter the printing and paper characteristics:

1 Choose Preferences from the File menu and Printing Inks Setup from the submenu. The Printing Inks Setup dialog box appears.

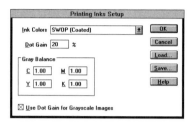

When you're doing your own work, you will change the values in this dialog box depending on the requirements of individual projects. For the lessons in *Classroom in a Book*, you will use the default settings.

2 Choose SWOP (Coated) from the Ink Colors pop-up menu.

Standard Web Offset Proofing (SWOP) inks printed on coated paper are the most commonly used inks in the United States. These inks differ slightly from those used in Europe.

3 Enter 20 for the Dot Gain.

Printed colors consist of a series of dots. *Dot gain* is a printing characteristic that causes dots to print larger than they should, producing darker tones or colors than expected. Different printers and papers have different dot gains.

4 Make sure that the Use Dot Gain for Grayscale Images option is selected, then click OK.

With your system calibrated, you're ready to begin working in Adobe Photoshop.

OPENING A FILE

Adobe Photoshop works with bitmapped, digitized images (that is, continuous-tone images that have been converted into a series of dots, or picture elements, called *pixels*). You can bring images into Adobe Photoshop by scanning a photograph, slide, or graphic; by capturing a video image; or by importing artwork created in drawing programs. You can also import previously digitized images—such as those produced by a digital camera or the Kodak™ PhotoCD process. For more information about the kinds of files you can use with Adobe Photoshop, see Lesson 11 in this book, and Chapter 2 in the *Adobe Photoshop User Guide.*

If Adobe Photoshop isn't running, start the program by double-clicking the application icon in the Adobe Photoshop directory.

To begin your first project, you need to open the CRAB.PSD file.

To open a file:

1 Choose Open from the File menu (or press Control+O). The Open dialog box appears so you can choose a file.

The *Classroom in a Book* files are stored in individual lesson directories. The files you'll use in this lesson are in the LESSON1 directory.

2 Open the Adobe Photoshop CIB directory, then open the LESSON1 directory.

3 Select the CRAB.PSD (extension) file and click OK.

The files used in *Classroom in a Book* were locked when they were originally created, therefore, a dialog box appears telling you that you will not be able to save any changes in this file. The files are locked so that users will not accidentally override

the original file name. This alert box will appear every time you open a file in this book. Simply click OK to continue.

4 Click OK or press the Enter key on the keyboard.

The CRAB.PSD file is in Photoshop 2.5 format—the default format for saved images. The crab image appears in a document window. When you start Adobe Photoshop, the menu bar and two palettes appear on the screen—the toolbox and the Brushes palette.

The toolbox contains selection tools, painting and editing tools, foreground and background color selection boxes, and viewing mode controls. You'll use the toolbox selection tools and the color selection boxes in this lesson. The painting and editing tools and the Brushes palette are explained in Lesson 2.

WORKING WITH SELECTIONS

Making a *selection* is the first step for almost all the work you'll do in Adobe Photoshop. You use the *selection tools* to isolate the part of the image you want to work on, then use the painting and editing tools or the menu commands to complete the action.

For example, to change the color in part of an image, you select the area and then use the Fill command. To create photomontages, you select part of one image and paste the selection into another image. To create special effects, you select an area and apply one or more filters. If you don't make a selection, the tools and commands affect the entire image. When you're color-correcting an image, for example, you often work without a selection.

To see how this works, you're going to experiment with a saved selection in the CRAB.PSD file.

To display the selection:

1 Choose Load Selection from the Select menu.

Look at the shell in the lower-left corner of the image. You see a series of "marching ants" around the edge of the shell. This is the *selection marquee* or *selection border*. Any action you take now affects only this selected area.

2 Choose Stylize from the Filter menu and Find Edges from the submenu.

Adobe Photoshop comes with many different filters that let you dramatically change the appearance of an image. You'll learn more about these filters in later lessons.

Applying the Stylize filter changes the selection, emphasizing the color contours in the shell. Notice that only the area within the selection changes.

Each image can have only one active selection at a time (although you can save several selections within one image). A single selection doesn't have to be contiguous; you can have several areas included in one selection.

Making a selection

Now that you understand how a selection works, you're going to make your own selection in the CRAB.PSD image. There are four selection tools in the toolbox.

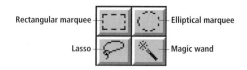

The *rectangular marquee tool* and the *elliptical marquee tool* allow you to select areas by dragging a selection marquee in the image. The *lasso tool* allows you to draw a freehand outline around an area. If you've used other drawing or painting programs, you're probably already familiar with these selection tools.

The *magic wand tool* allows you to select parts of an image based on the color similarities of adjacent pixels. This tool is useful for selecting odd-shaped areas (such as a yellow flower), without having to trace a complex outline using the lasso.

Adobe Photoshop also includes a fifth selection tool—the *pen tool* located on the Paths palette. The pen tool lets you draw precise *paths* of straight and curved lines, which you can then convert into selections. You'll learn how to use the pen tool in Lesson 4.

Making an area-based selection

For your first selection, you're going to use the elliptical marquee tool to select a lemon slice.

To select the lemon:

1 Click the elliptical marquee tool in the toolbox and move the pointer into the image area. Notice that the pointer turns into a crosshair.

2 Click the upper-left corner of the bottom lemon slice and drag down and to the right.

The marquee around the previous selection of the shell disappears (remember, you can have only one active selection at a time). A new marquee begins drawing the selection border from the corner where you clicked. However, this doesn't produce exactly the selection you want.

Click point　　　　　*Resulting selection*

3 Choose Undo Marquee from the Edit menu (or press Control+Z).

The Undo command always reverses your last action. In this case, the selection border disappears. Because this command allows you to change your mind, feel free to experiment while you're learning Adobe Photoshop. Keep in mind, however, only your *last action* is undone by this command. (In the next lesson, you'll learn how to use the Revert command, which reverses *all the actions* you've performed in the current work session.)

4 Hold down the Alt key, position the crosshair in the white center of the lemon, and drag again.

Holding down the Alt key starts the marquee from the center. This makes it easier to select the lemon shape.

Click point with Alt Key　　　*Resulting selection*

Duplicating a selection

Now that you've got the lemon selected, you're going to add a third lemon slice to the image.

Your first inclination is probably to drag the selection to the new location. Go ahead and try this now.

TIP: WHEN STARTING
A SELECTION MARQUEE
FROM THE CENTER,
BE SURE TO RELEASE
THE MOUSE BEFORE
YOU RELEASE THE
ALT KEY.

1 Click anywhere in the selected area and drag the lemon slice down and to the right.

You probably expected the original lemon slice to stay in its location, and a new lemon slice to appear as you dragged. But, instead, you're left with an empty white space! What you see is the *background color* of the image. In Adobe Photoshop, dragging a selection moves the actual pixels, leaving an area that is automatically filled with the background color.

2 Choose Undo Move from the Edit menu to return the selection to its original place.

The lemon slice is still selected. To duplicate a selection and move it to a new location, you copy the selection, paste the copy into the image, then drag the copy.

3 Choose Copy from the Edit menu (or press Control+C). The lemon slice is copied to the Clipboard.

4 Choose Paste from the Edit menu (or press Control+V).

Although it appears that nothing has changed in the image, a copy of the lemon slice has been pasted directly over the original selection.

5 Drag the copy down and to the right.

Don't worry about the exact location or if there is some extra space around the lemon slice. The important thing is that you've just had your first taste of how easy it is to manipulate images in Adobe Photoshop.

Pasting a selection makes it the current selection. You can see that the selection border is now around the lemon slice that you dragged.

6 Choose Save As from the File menu.

7 Open your Projects directory.

If you haven't created this directory, see the "Getting Started" section at the beginning of this book for instructions on storing your saved files.

8 Name the file CRAB2.PSD and save it in the Projects directory.

Making a color-based selection

When you used the elliptical marquee tool, you selected the pixels in a specific area. The magic wand tool works in a slightly different way—it selects adjacent pixels based on their color. For your next selection, you're going to use the magic wand tool to select the crab.

To select the crab:

1 Click the magic wand tool in the toolbox and move the pointer into the image area. Notice that the pointer changes into a wand.

2 Position the wand in the shell under the top claw and click.

About half of the crab shell is selected (the lighter areas in the shell, the legs, and the claws are not selected). Your selection might be slightly different, depending on exactly where you placed the magic wand.

Notice that the selection border around the lemon slice disappears. This is because each Adobe Photoshop image can have only one active selection at a time. Usually when you begin a new selection border, the previous selection disappears. There are several ways, however, to *add* to a selection.

Growing a selection

One way to increase a color-based selection is to use the Grow and Similar commands from the Select menu. The Grow command selects *adjacent* pixels of the same color. The Similar command selects the same color pixels wherever they appear in the image.

To increase a selection based on color:

1 Choose Grow from the Select menu (or press Control+G).

The selection increases so that most of the shell and parts of the legs and claws are selected. The lighter-yellow sections of the crab (and the red areas that are not adjacent to the current selection) are still unselected.

Both the magic wand tool and the Grow and Similar commands select pixels that are alike in color. How similar the color must be is determined by the *tolerance* setting in the Magic Wand Options dialog box. A higher tolerance selects pixels with a wider color range; a lower tolerance limits the selection to pixels that are very close in color.

2 Double-click the magic wand tool in the toolbox. The Magic Wand Options dialog box appears. Increase the Tolerance setting to 45 and click OK.

Increasing the tolerance will add the lighter red and yellow pixels to the selection when you next use the command.

3 Choose Grow again.

Now you've selected almost all of the crab. There are still some small sections in the middle of the shell and the tips of the claws that need to be included.

Adding to and subtracting from a selection

Using the Grow command is a convenient way to add incrementally to a selection when there are clear color distinctions. To make more precise adjustments to a selection border, you use the lasso tool.

Remember, each click of a selection tool normally starts a new selection. When you want to add to or subtract from a selection, you hold down the Shift key (to add) or the Control key (to subtract) as you enclose areas using the lasso.

To add to a selection:

1 Click the lasso tool in the toolbox and move the pointer into the image area. If you're outside the selected area, the pointer turns into a lasso.

2 Hold down the Shift key and draw a lasso around the areas on the crab's back that aren't selected.

Start drawing from within the current selection and be sure to start and end the lasso at the same point. If you don't, Adobe Photoshop will draw a connecting selection marquee between the point at which you began drawing and the last point.

If your selection disappears, you probably forgot to hold down the Shift key before using the lasso tool. Choose Undo from the Edit menu to return to your previous selection, and try again. Your selection should now include all of the crab's back.

Just to experiment, try subtracting part of the shell from the selection.

To subtract from a selection:

1 With the lasso tool selected, hold down the Control key and draw a lasso around the center of the shell.

You can see that the area you enclosed is no longer part of the selection.

2 Choose Undo Lasso from the Edit menu to delete your last action.

MAGNIFYING THE IMAGE

To make selecting the claws easier, you're going to zoom in before you continue adding to the selection. The title bar tells you that, right now, you're looking at a 1:1 view of the image.

In Adobe Photoshop, the view ratio is 1 monitor pixel to 1 image pixel, not the actual physical size of the image. Images are sometimes displayed at a resolution of 72 lines per inch (lpi), which is a common Windows monitor resolution. Check your own monitor resolution because it may vary based on the manufacturer. An image with a resolution higher than 72 lpi appears bigger on the screen than its actual size. For example, a 3-inch by 4-inch image with a resolution of 144 pixels per inch (which is approximately twice the monitor resolution) takes up a 6-inch by 8-inch area on the screen when viewed at a 1:1 ratio. The same image with a resolution of 300 (four times the monitor resolution) would appear to be 24 inches by 32 inches.

You use the *zoom tool* to increase and decrease the image's view ratio. Changing the view ratio modifies how the image appears on the screen, but it doesn't change the actual size of the image.

To increase the magnification of the view:

1 Click the zoom tool in the toolbox and move the pointer into the image. Notice that the pointer turns into a magnifying glass with a plus sign.

2 Position the magnifying glass in the black area between the two claws, and click.

1:1 view

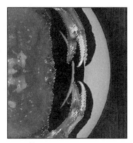
2:1 view

The image is enlarged by one order of magnification. The title bar now shows a 2:1 view ratio. Each click of the zoom tool increases the magnification by a factor of 2.

Increasing the magnification makes it easier to add the claw tips to the selection.

To add the top claw to the selection:

1 Click the lasso tool in the toolbox.

2 Since you are adding to the selection, *hold down the Shift key* while you use the lasso to trace the top claw tip. Be sure you start dragging the lasso inside the current selection border, and close the lasso at the same point that you started it.

Don't worry if your selection border isn't perfect; the general shape of the claw is all that's important for this selection.

3 Continue to use the lasso tool to add any small unselected areas within the top claw.

If you accidentally include part of the plate or background in the selection, use the Control key with the lasso tool to subtract the unwanted areas.

Moving around in the image

When you're working in a magnified view, you can't see the entire image. One way to move around in the image is to use the standard scroll arrows and scroll bars. Another way to scroll is to drag sections of the image into view using the *hand tool.*

To add the bottom claw tip to the selection:

1 Click the hand tool in the toolbox and move the pointer into the image area. Notice that the pointer turns into a hand.

2 Position the hand in the black area between the claws and drag upward to display all of the bottom claw.

3 Click the lasso tool, then *hold down the Shift key* and use the lasso to outline the claw tip and include the areas within the claw that aren't selected.

Again, don't worry about exactness. If you're unhappy with the outline, choose Undo Lasso and retrace the area.

Once you've added the claw, you'll notice that the selection border is not quite correct where the bottom claw intersects the shell. You need to smooth out the selection border. Zooming in again will help you to see this area more clearly.

4 Choose Zoom In from the Window menu (or press Control+plus).

The Zoom In command does the same thing as clicking the zoom tool, except that the magnification factor is 1 instead of 2. The view ratio is now 3:1.

5 If necessary, use the hand tool to move down in the image until you can see the intersection of the crab back and claw.

6 Use the lasso tool to add or subtract areas to correct the selection border.

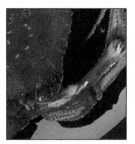 

Adding a selection   *New selection*

Zooming out in an image

Using the zoom tool with the Alt key allows you to reduce the view ratio. Each click of the Alt+zoom tool combination reduces the magnification by a factor of 2.

1 Click the zoom tool and hold down the Alt key as you move the pointer into the image area. Notice that the pointer appears as a magnifying glass with a minus sign.

2 Click to reduce the image magnification to 2:1.

3 Choose Zoom Out from the Window menu (or press Control+minus).

The Zoom Out command does the same thing as the Alt+zoom tool combination. The image view is now back to its original 1:1 ratio.

Using zoom shortcuts

Here are some techniques you can use to zoom in, zoom out, or move around in an image *while you're using another tool.*

To try out the zoom shortcuts:

1 Click one of the selection tools.

2 Press Control+spacebar.

The zoom-in magnifying glass appears. Pressing Control+spacebar has the same effect as clicking the zoom tool or choosing Zoom In from the Window menu.

3 Release both keys and press Alt+spacebar.

The zoom-out magnifying glass appears. Pressing Alt+spacebar has the same effect as holding down the Alt key and clicking the zoom tool or choosing Zoom Out from the Window menu.

4 Release the Alt key so you're holding down only the spacebar.

The hand tool appears. Pressing the spacebar has the same effect as clicking the hand tool.

5 Use one of the shortcuts to zoom in or zoom out, then double-click the zoom tool.

You are quickly returned to the 1:1 view of this image (this works no matter what the magnification is).

One convenient way to use these shortcuts is to put your ring finger on the Control key, your middle finger on the Alt key, and your index finger on the spacebar. When all three fingers are pressed down, the zoom-out icon appears. If you lift your

ring finger and release the Control key, the zoom-in icon appears. If you lift your ring and middle fingers so that only the spacebar is pressed, the hand icon appears. Once you get used to these key combinations, you'll be amazed at how quickly you can move to exactly the part of the image you want to work in.

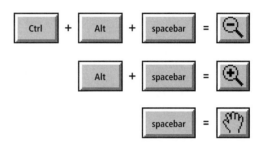

Fine-tuning the selection

Using the selection and magnification techniques you've learned, you're now ready to make final adjustments to the crab selection.

To select the rest of the crab:

1 While you're in the 1:1 view, note any areas in the crab that are still unselected.

Pay particular attention to the back of the shell and the crab legs on the left side. If you see any small areas enclosed by marquees, these areas need to be added to the selection. You might also want to check the outside edges to see if the selection border makes any noticeable detours into the background.

2 Use the lasso tool and the zoom techniques to adjust the selection border until you're satisfied with the results.

Small imperfections aren't important. Just have fun trying out the tools, commands, and shortcuts. When your selection border resembles the following illustration, you're ready to move on.

SAVING A SELECTION

You can see that making a selection, especially one as intricate as the crab, can take some time. When you think you might use a complex selection again, it's wise to save it. *If you don't save a selection, it is lost when you begin making your next selection.*

At the beginning of this lesson you loaded a pre-saved selection of the shell. Now, you're going to save your crab selection, since you'll use it in the next lesson.

To save a selection:

1 Choose Save Selection from the Select menu, and New from the submenu.

Although you won't notice any change in the image, your selection has been automatically stored in a special part of the file called a *channel*. (You'll learn how to display and use channels in Lesson 4.)

You chose New from the submenu since the shell selection is already stored in channel #4. Adobe Photoshop automatically creates a new channel (and names it #5) to save the selection. In Lesson 4, you'll learn how to give channels descriptive names.

Even though it's saved, the crab is still the current selection. To verify that the crab selection has been saved, you're going to deselect it, then load the saved selection.

2 Choose None from the Select menu (or press Control+D).

The selection border disappears and there is no current selection in the image.

3 Choose Load Selection from the Select menu, and #5 from the submenu.

The selection is loaded and the selection border again appears around the crab. If you want to try this a few more times, choose the Load Selection command again and alternate between loading the shell selection (#4) and the crab selection (#5).

4 Choose None from the Select menu to deselect your last loaded selection.

The saved selection can be reused in this image as many times as you want. However, to be sure the selection is available the next time you open this file, you must also save the file.

5 Choose Save As from the File menu.

6 Open the Projects directory and save the image as CRAB3.PSD.

USING THE FOREGROUND AND BACKGROUND COLORS

Adobe Photoshop uses the *foreground color* to paint, to fill selections, and as the beginning color for gradient fills. The *background color* is used when you erase; to fill in the original location of a moved, cut, or deleted selection; and as the ending color for gradient fills.

The default foreground color is black and the default background color is white. The current foreground and background colors are shown in the *color selection boxes* in the toolbox. Clicking the *switch colors icon* reverses the colors. Clicking the *default colors icon* returns the foreground color to black and the background color to white.

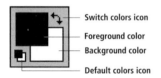

— Switch colors icon
— Foreground color
— Background color
— Default colors icon

In this lesson, you're going to change the foreground color using the Color Picker. The Color Picker lets you choose colors from a broad color spectrum.

To change the foreground color:

1 Click the foreground color selection box in the toolbox. The Color Picker dialog box appears.

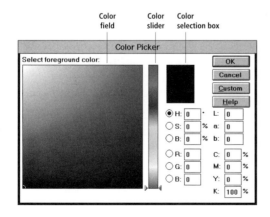

Color field   Color slider   Color selection box

The current foreground color is indicated by a circle marker in the bottom-left corner of the color field and is shown in the Color Picker's color selection box. The Color Picker has a number of settings that let you choose colors from different color models (such as RGB and CMYK), or designate colors by numeric values. See the *Adobe Photoshop User Guide* for a complete explanation of the Color Picker.

2 Drag the triangles to the red color at the top of the color slider. (If red is not showing in your Color Picker, be sure the H button under the color selection box is selected.)

Notice that the circle marker remains in the same location.

3 Click the upper-right corner of the color field to choose a bright red color.

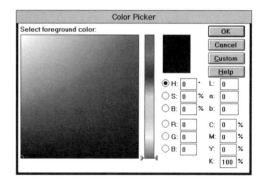

The new foreground color appears in the top of the Color Picker's color selection box (the old foreground color appears in the bottom half of the box).

4 Click OK to close the Color Picker.

The foreground color selection box in the toolbox displays the new foreground color.

You can use the standard Windows Color Picker instead of the Adobe Color Picker to designate new colors by changing the setting in the Adobe Photoshop General Preferences dialog box. See the *Adobe Photoshop User Guide* for more information.

FILLING A SELECTION

As the final task in this lesson, you're going to use the new foreground color to fill a selection. In the final image, you want to create a new red background—this means that you want to fill everything but the crab.

To fill the background:

1 Choose Load Selection from the Select menu and #5 from the submenu to load the crab selection.

2 Choose Inverse from the Select menu.

The selection now encompasses everything that was not previously selected—that is, the entire image except for the crab itself. At first glance, you might not think anything has changed, since the selection border is still around the crab. But notice that the outside of the image also contains a selection border. It's the area between the marquees that is selected.

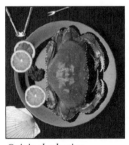 

Original selection   *Inverse selection*

3 Choose Fill from the Edit menu.

The Fill dialog box appears. By default, the Fill command uses the foreground color for the fill (later you'll learn how to fill selections using a pattern).

4 Make sure the Foreground Color option is selected, the Opacity is set to 100 percent, and the Mode is set to Normal.

5 Click OK to fill the selection.

The background becomes a bright red.

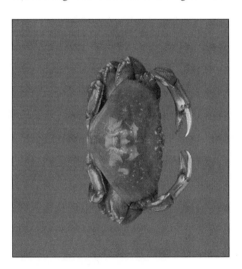

6 Choose Save from the File menu (or press Control+S).

And there you are! In just a short time you've transformed this crab into a dramatically different image that bears only a slight resemblance to the original image. You're well on your way to understanding the excitement and adventure of image editing with Adobe Photoshop.

LE MONDE

B

Gourmet *Visions*

PAINTING AND EDITING

Lesson 2: Painting and Editing

esson 2 acquaints you with the painting and editing tools in the toolbox. The painting and editing tools allow you to make changes in images, from subtle corrections to dramatic artistic effects.

In this lesson, you'll paint and edit the selection you saved in Lesson 1 and add type to the new image. It should take you about one hour to complete this lesson.

In this lesson, you'll learn how to do the following:

- use the Brushes palette

- sample color with the eyedropper tool

- paint with the pencil, paintbrush, and airbrush tools

- use the Colors palette

- blend colors using the smudge tool

- change the painting and editing modes

- clone areas using the rubber stamp tool

- crop an image

- increase the canvas size of an image

- create a gradient fill

- add type with the type tool

At the end of this lesson you'll have a compelling, impressionistic cookbook cover, sure to entice any seafood lover.

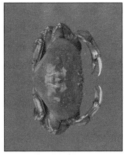

Beginning image (NEWCRAB.PSD)

Ending image (CBOOK.PSD)

WORKING WITH PALETTES

Adobe Photoshop has five palettes—the toolbox, the Brushes palette, the Channels palette, the Colors palette, the Info palette, and the Paths palette. At one time or another, you'll use most of these palettes in conjunction with the painting and editing tools.

The toolbox and Brushes palette open automatically when you start Adobe Photoshop. To display the other palettes, you choose their Show command from the Window menu. You can also display palettes using the preassigned function key shortcuts. This option is available on extended keyboards only. See the *Adobe Photoshop User Guide* for more information.

As you read along, try out these palette characteristics on the Brushes palette:

1 All the Adobe Photoshop palettes are *floating*. To move a palette anywhere on the screen, drag its title bar. Floating palettes always appear in front of any images you have on the screen.

2 All the palettes have pop-up menus. To choose a command, click the Control menu button in the upper left corner of the pallette window to display the menu.

3 All of the palettes are *collapsible.* To increase your work space, click the zoom box at the right side of the palette's title bar. Click the zoom box again to display the entire palette.

4 The Brushes, Channels, Colors, and Paths palettes can be resized. To make a palette larger or smaller, drag the size box in the lower-right corner of the palette.

5 To hide individual palettes, choose their Hide command from the Window menu or click the palette's close box at the left side of the title bar.

6 Press Tab to hide or display all the open palettes. Pressing the Tab key is the only way to hide and redisplay the toolbox.

In this lesson, you'll use the Brushes palette and the Colors palette. The Channels and Paths palettes are covered in Lesson 4, and the Info palette is discussed in Lesson 7.

BEGINNING THIS LESSON

At the beginning of each of the remaining *Classroom in a Book* lessons, you'll find a section just like this that tells you how to set up your windows and palettes before you begin working.

Setting up the palettes

To begin this lesson, only the toolbox and Brushes palette should be open on your desktop. If any other palettes are open, close or hide them now.

Opening your working file

To start this lesson, you need to open the NEWCRAB.PSD file and have the crab selection visible.

To open the file:

1 Open the Adobe Photoshop CIB directory, then open the LESSON2 directory.

2 Double-click the NEWCRAB.PSD file.

If you prefer, you can use the CRAB3.PSD file you saved in your Projects directory at the end of Lesson 1.

3 Choose Load Selection from the Select menu and #5 from the submenu.

This is how your screen should look.

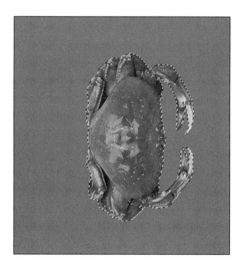

In this lesson, you're using the crab selection as a *mask*— that is, you're going to use the shape of the crab to limit the painting area. In order to see your painting efforts more clearly, you're going to delete the crab selection, leaving a clean white area within the selection border to paint on.

4 Click the *default colors icon* in the toolbox to return the foreground color to black and the background color to white.

Remember, when you cut, delete, or move a selection, the area is filled with the background color.

5 Press the Backspace or Delete key. If you prefer, you can choose Cut from the Edit menu (or press Control+X).

This is how your screen should look.

Opening the reference file

This lesson allows you some leeway in the settings and colors you'll use to paint the crab. You may find it helpful to open the final version of this image included in the *Classroom in a Book* files. Use this final image for reference as you paint your own interpretation of the crab.

To open the final image:

1 Choose Open from the File menu and select the CBOOK.PSD file in the LESSON2 directory.

Since you won't be working in this image, it doesn't need to take up so much room on your screen.

2 Zoom out to decrease the view ratio.

3 Drag the window to the upper-right corner of your screen.

You can put the image in a different location if that feels more natural for you. Remember to leave space on the screen for additional palettes.

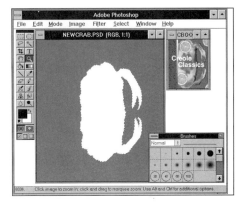

Displaying the rulers

Since you're going to be painting in a specific location in this window, you'll probably find it helpful to display the window rulers. When the rulers are visible, moving a pointer inside the window displays position markers on the rulers.

To display the rulers:

1 Choose Show Rulers from the Window menu (or press Control+R).

The rulers appear along the left edge and at the top of the CBOOK.PSD window.

2 Click the NEWCRAB.PSD (or CRAB3.PSD) window to make it active, then choose Show Rulers again.

As you can see, each window has its own ruler setting. Ruler settings apply to the current work session only; you must redisplay the rulers when you next open a file. When you want to turn off the rulers, choose Hide Rulers from the Window menu (or press Control+R).

USING THE PAINTING AND EDITING TOOLS

It's difficult to differentiate the painting and editing tools. In reality, you use a combination of all the tools when you're creating or editing an image.

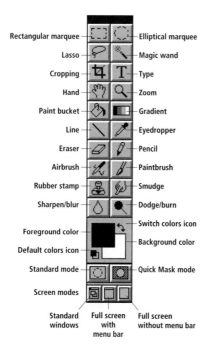

In general, the *pencil tool*, the *airbrush tool*, the *paintbrush tool*, the *line tool*, and the *rubber stamp tool* are referred to as the painting tools. Sometimes the *paint bucket tool* and the *gradient fill tool* are also included in this category.

The *eraser tool*, the *cropping tool*, the *smudge tool*, the *blur/sharpen tool*, and the *dodge/burn tool* are referred to as the editing tools. The *type tool* is in a category by itself. In this lesson, you'll use most of these tools to paint the crab selection.

PAINTING WITH THE PENCIL TOOL

When you paint in a pixel program, you change the color of individual pixels. Depending on the opacity or pressure you've chosen for the painting tool, you can completely obscure the original color or you can let part of the original color show through.

The number of colors you can work with depends on the system you're using. An 8-bit color system, for example, can display a maximum of 256 colors simultaneously; 24-bit or 32-bit systems can display more than 16 million colors.

To begin painting, you're going to use the *pencil tool*, which uses hard-edged strokes to paint with the foreground color. To make painting easier, you're going to zoom in first.

To paint with the pencil tool:

1 Click the zoom tool in the toolbox.

2 Drag a rectangle around the top claw.

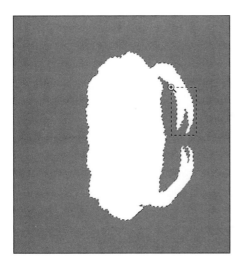

As you drag, a marquee appears that indicates the area you're magnifying. This technique, called *marquee-zooming*, is useful for magnifying a very specific part of an image. Your view ratio should be 3:1 or 4:1.

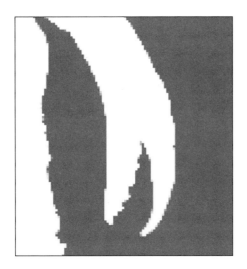

3 Click the pencil tool in the toolbox and move the pointer into the image area. Notice that the pointer changes into a pencil.

Once you have chosen the pencil tool, a box appears around the top-left brush in the Brushes palette. This is the default brush for the pencil tool (each tool has its own default brush). The Brushes palette for the pencil tool contains hard-edged brushes of various sizes. The brushes in the third row are too big to show visually; the number in the circle tells you the brush diameter.

4 Check that the Opacity slider at the top of the Brushes palette is set to 100 percent (if it isn't, drag the slider all the way to the right).

5 Use the pencil tool to begin tracing along the edge of the claw. (Your foreground color should be black.)

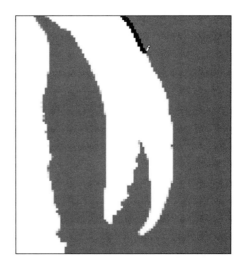

Working in this magnification lets you actually see the individual pixels as they are filled in. Because the crab is selected, you can't unintentionally stray into the red background, since painting tools only affect the currently selected area in an image.

Don't worry about the precise location or width of the areas you paint. The exact appearance of the selection isn't important. The point of all the exercises in this lesson is to help you become familiar with the painting and editing tools, not to create an exact replica of the final image.

6 Click the fourth brush from the left in the top row of the Brushes palette.

7 Zoom out once and paint along the inside of the crab shell. (Did you remember to use the Alt+spacebar shortcut?)

This thicker brush fills in a larger area with a single pass.

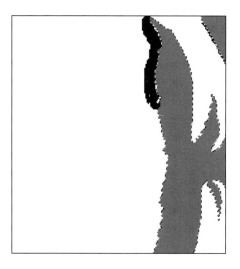

USING THE TOOL POINTERS

When you move the pencil tool into an image, the pointer turns into a pencil tool. Sometimes, when you're using the pencil tool (and the other painting and editing tools) it's difficult to know exactly where the painting will begin. Each of the tool pointers has a *hot spot*—the spot where the action begins. When you want to edit or paint with real precision, you might want to turn the pointer into this *hot spot* crosshair. Using the intersection of the crosshair, you can focus on the area you want to paint or edit.

To paint using the crosshair:

1 Scroll down until the bottom claw is visible.

2 Move the pencil tool to the edge of the crab shell and press the Caps Lock key.

The pencil turns into a crosshair.

3 Try using one or two other brush sizes as you use the pencil to paint with precision along the crab shell and claw edges.

4 Release the Caps Lock key to return to the pencil pointer.

Use your reference image as a guide. To get a better perspective on your painting, return to a 1:1 view occasionally to see the entire image, then zoom in to paint specific areas. (Use the shortcut of double-clicking the zoom tool to return to a 1:1 view instantly.)

While you're painting, you can use Undo to delete the last brush stroke.

5 Continue painting (turning the crosshair off and on) until your selection resembles the following illustration.

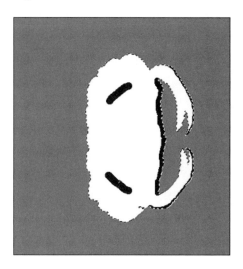

6 Return to the 1:1 view ratio when you've finished painting.

7 Choose Save As and open your Projects directory.

8 Save this file as PAINTED1.PSD.

SAMPLING A NEW FOREGROUND COLOR

When the color you want to use for the foreground color is in an open image, you can use the *eyedropper tool* to sample the color.

1 Click the eyedropper tool in the toolbox and move the pointer into the image area. Notice that the pointer turns into an eyedropper.

2 Position the eyedropper over the red in the image and click.

The foreground color selection box in the toolbox turns to red.

PAINTING WITH THE PAINTBRUSH TOOL

Now, you're going to use the *paintbrush tool* to paint with the red color. The paintbrush paints soft-edged strokes using the foreground color.

1 Click the paintbrush tool in the toolbox and move the pointer into the image area. Notice that the pointer turns into a paintbrush.

When the paintbrush tool is selected, the Brushes palette contains soft-edged brushes. The default brush for the paintbrush tool is somewhat larger than the default brush for the pencil tool.

2 Choose the fifth brush from the left in the second row of the Brushes palette.

3 Paint a circle on the back of the crab.

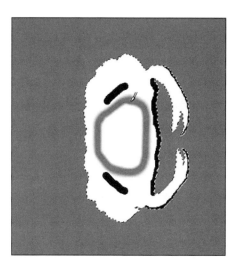

The area that you're painting is the undercoat for the other colors you'll add to the crab.

4 Click the second brush from the right in the top row of the Brushes palette.

5 Press the Caps Lock key to turn on the tool's hot spot, and continue painting to see the effects of a larger brush with a harder edge.

6 Press the Caps Lock key again to return to the paintbrush pointer.

Creating a new brush

Adobe Photoshop doesn't limit you to using only the brushes available on the Brushes palette. You can easily create new brushes for use with any tool.

1 Click the Control menu button in the upper-left corner of the Brushes palette to display the pop-up menu, and choose New Brush.

The New Brush dialog box appears (the values in the box are the settings for the currently selected brush).

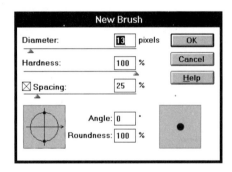

2 Enter 20 for the Diameter and 5 for the Hardness. You can either drag the slider or type in numbers to enter the new values.

The diameter controls the size of the brush. The hardness is a measurement of the hard center of the brush and is a percentage of the brush diameter. See the *Adobe Photoshop User Guide* for information on the other settings in this dialog box.

As you enter new settings, the preview box in the lower-right corner of the dialog box shows you the new brush.

3 Click OK to create the new brush.

Look at the bottom row of the Brushes palette. The new brush appears in the next available space on the palette. If you add several brushes to a palette, you can resize the palette to see more than four rows of brushes. You can also use the Delete Brush command in the palette pop-up menu to get rid of brushes you no longer need.

4 Use your new brush to paint the rest of the center of the shell.

5 Choose a smaller brush to paint red inside the claws and the claw tips.

You may want to zoom in to paint the detailed areas. Feel free to add your own interpretative touches.

6 Save the file.

USING THE COLORS PALETTE

To continue painting, you're going to choose a new foreground color. You've already learned two ways to change the foreground color; you can choose a new color from the Color Picker, or you can use the eyedropper to sample a color in the image. The Colors palette provides a third way of selecting foreground and background colors. You can also mix custom colors in the Colors palette.

To choose a color from the Colors palette:

1 Choose Show Colors from the Window menu. The Colors palette appears.

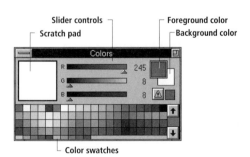

The large rectangle on the left of the Colors palette is the *scratch pad*, which you'll use in a minute to mix a new color. The color selection boxes on the right show the current foreground and background colors. The sliders in between display the *color values* of the foreground color: approximately 250 for the red (R), 4 for the green (G), and 16 for the blue (B). You can ignore these sliders at the moment; you will learn more about them in Lesson 4.

Along the bottom of the palette are the 90 colors of the default Adobe Photoshop palette. Like the Brushes palette, you can customize the Colors palette by adding and deleting colors.

2 Drag the Colors palette to the lower left corner of your screen.

Drag the palette by its title bar to move it.

3 Click the yellow color swatch in the top row.

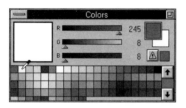

As you move the pointer over the color swatches, it turns into an eyedropper. When you click, the new color appears in the foreground color selection box in both the Colors palette and the toolbox.

4 Click the third brush from the left in the second row of the Brushes palette (the paintbrush tool should still be selected).

5 Use this fine brush to outline areas along the outside of the red circle and to embellish the claw tips.

6 Use a finer brush to paint the yellow in the claw tips.

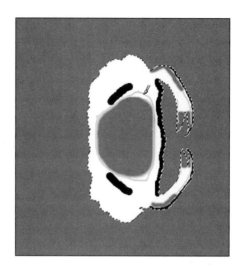

7 As you continue to paint, switch back and forth between the pencil and the paintbrush tools.

When you use multiple tools, Adobe Photoshop remembers the last brush you were using for each specific tool. The last used brush is automatically reselected when you return to a tool.

Changing the brush opacity

The Opacity slider in the Brushes palette controls the transparency of the paint. For the paintbrush and pencil tools, the default opacity setting is 100 percent. Since you've been painting with 100 percent opaque paint, the red areas you've painted over with the yellow paint have been completely obscured. Lowering the opacity setting makes the paint you apply more transparent.

1 Drag the Opacity slider to 50 percent.

2 Paint over some more of the red areas with the yellow paint.

You can see that the paint now takes on an orange tone as the red and yellow pixels overlap.

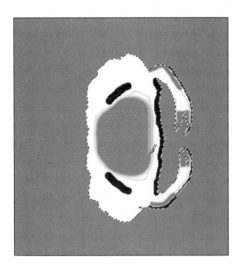

3 Click the middle green in the third row of the Colors palette.

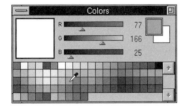

4 Do some improvisational painting as you vary the opacity setting and brushes.

Stop when your image has enough green (you can always come back later and add more green or eliminate some green with another color).

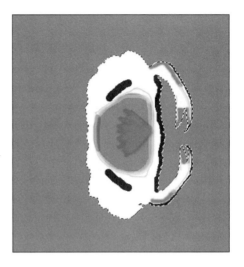

5 Save the file when you've finished painting.

Mixing a custom color

The scratch pad on the left side of the Colors palette lets you use the painting tools to mix colors. You can use any of the painting tools to paint on the scratch pad. To eliminate colors, use the eraser.

To mix a color:

1 Click the blue swatch in the middle of the third row in the Colors palette.

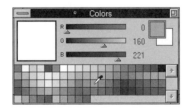

2 Set the opacity to 100 percent, click the second brush from the left in the second row of the Brushes palette, and use the paintbrush to paint in the scratch pad.

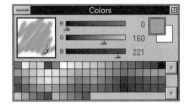

3 Click the gray swatch to the right of the white swatch in the first row of the Colors palette, set the opacity to 36 percent, and paint over the blue in the scratch pad.

4 Click the red swatch in the top row of the Colors palette, set the opacity to 9 percent, and paint in the scratch pad again.

This red tint changes the color slightly but you should be able to detect the difference. If you can't, increase the opacity a little, and paint again.

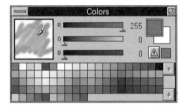

5 Hold down the Alt key and sample the custom color in the scratch pad to make it the foreground color.

When you have another tool selected, holding down the Alt key automatically displays the eye-dropper so you can sample a color.

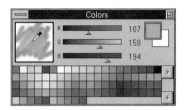

This technique works in the image area, too. Using this shortcut, you can select a new foreground color without switching the tools in the toolbox.

Adding a color to the Colors palette

Since you will use this color several times to finish painting the crab, you are going to add it to the Colors palette now.

To add a color to the Colors palette:

1 Be sure the blue custom color is the foreground color.

2 Move the pointer over the empty white space in the bottom row of the Colors palette. Notice that the pointer turns into the paint bucket tool.

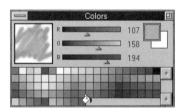

3 Click to add the color to the Colors palette.

PAINTING WITH THE AIRBRUSH TOOL

 The *airbrush tool* lays down a diffused spray of the foreground color.

To paint using the airbrush:

1 Click the airbrush tool in the toolbox and move the pointer into the image area. Notice that the pointer turns into an airbrush.

The Brushes palette changes to reflect the default settings for the airbrush. The brush size is large, 35 pixels in diameter. The opacity setting is replaced by a pressure setting with a value of 50 percent. You specify a high pressure percentage for a strong effect and a low percentage for a more subtle effect.

2 Begin painting with your custom blue color in a white area of the shell.

3 Select a smaller brush, and change the Pressure to 100 percent to paint the blue areas in the bottom claw and leg.

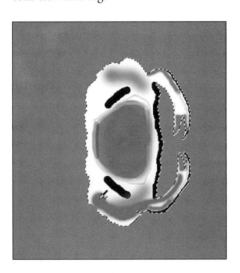

Changing the fade-out rate

Up to this point, all your paint strokes have been even along their entire length. To make the stroke look more like a real brush stroke, you're going to change the airbrush *fade-out rate*. The fade-out rate determines how many pixels are colored with each stroke before the paint fades out completely. The higher the fade-out rate, the longer the paint flows before it fades out. You can make the paint fade from the foreground color to transparent, or from the foreground color to the background color.

1 Double-click the airbrush tool and set the Fade-out option in the Airbrush Options dialog box to 20 (the To Transparent option is automatically selected).

2 Zoom in on the white area in the upper claw and back (or any white area you want to use) and use the airbrush tool with a fairly narrow brush to paint one stroke.

3 Change the Fade-out option to 40 and paint a second stroke of the same length next to the first one.

You can see that the first stroke, with the lower fade-out rate, becomes transparent first.

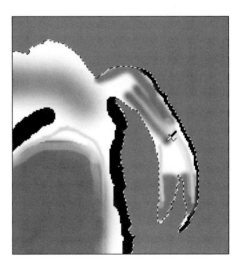

TIP: YOU CAN USE THE KEYBOARD TO CHANGE THE OPACITY OR PRES-SURE SETTING. PRESS 1 TO SET THE OPACITY OR PRESSURE TO 10%, PRESS 5 TO CHANGE THE SETTING TO 50% AND SO ON. PRESS ZERO TO SET 100% OPACITY OR PRESSURE.

4 Display the Airbrush Options dialog box again, change the Fade-out to 60, and click the To Background option.

5 In the Colors palette, select the background color selection box.

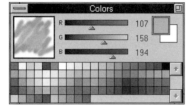

In the Colors palette, the currently selected color selection box is outlined.

6 Click the bright pink in the first row of the Colors palette to set a new background color.

7 Zoom out, and starting in the middle of the shell (in a white area), stroke upward.

As you finish the stroke, the paint fades out to pink, the current background color.

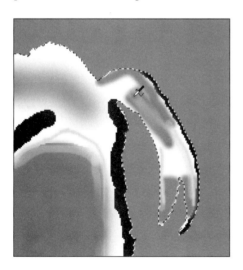

8 Change the Pressure and Fade-out rates as you stroke the blue paint toward the green in the center of the crab shell. (In addition to the airbrush, the pencil and paintbrush tools also have options for fade-out in their dialog boxes.)

9 Use the pencil, paintbrush, and airbrush tools with different brushes to paint the rest of the crab.

Try varying combinations of opacity, pressure, and fade-out rates. Don't forget to hold down the Caps Lock key when you want to paint with pinpoint accuracy. You can use the final image as a guide, or you can let your imagination run wild.

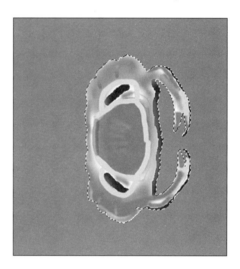

10 When you've finished painting, return the airbrush Fade-out rates to 0 for all three tools, then save the file.

SMUDGING A SELECTION

 As a final step in painting the crab, you're going to use the *smudge tool*. The smudge tool simulates the action of dragging a finger through wet paint. The tool picks up color from the starting point of the stroke and pushes it in the direction you drag. By varying the pressure in the Brushes palette, you can change the force of the smudge.

To use the smudge tool:

1 Zoom in so you can see the effect of the smudging more easily.

2 Click the smudge tool in the toolbox and move into the image area. Notice that the pointer turns into a finger (smudging is like the finger-painting you did in kindergarten).

3 Start in the green area of the claw and move into the blue paint (if you don't have blue next to green, use any two colors).

By default, the pressure setting for the smudge tool is 50 percent, so the two colors are about equally blended.

4 Vary the Pressure and the brush size as you continue to smudge.

Smudging allows you to create some very interesting effects. Stroke sharp lines with a fine brush to create streaks of color, or use a circular motion to create a swirl effect as you smudge. Your crab should be beginning to take on an abstract quality.

5 Save this file as PAINTED2.PSD.

Using the painting and editing modes

The Brushes palette contains one more setting that you use with the painting and editing tools. To the left of the opacity/pressure setting is a pop-up menu that currently reads **Normal**. This is the Mode pop-up menu. The *painting and editing modes* control which pixels are affected as you paint.

When the default Normal mode is active (as it has been up to now), each pixel you paint or edit changes. The amount of change depends on the tool's opacity, pressure, or fade-out settings. Changing the painting mode determines whether or not a pixel is affected in any way when paint is applied over it. See the *Adobe Photoshop User Guide* for information on all the painting and editing modes.

To use a different painting mode:

1 Scroll to the right edge of the crab back (or any place where you have a dark color and a lighter color near each other).

2 Choose Darken from the Mode pop-up menu.

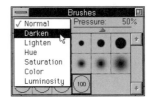

3 Make sure the Pressure is set to 100 percent. Then, starting from the light area, smudge into the darker area.

The Darken mode affects only pixels that are lighter than the beginning color. The smudge is apparent in the lighter areas, but does not affect the darker pixels since they are darker than the pixels you started the smudge with.

TIP: TO GET THE SOFTENED EFFECTS AROUND THE CLAWS AND LEGS, CHOOSE NONE FROM THE SELECT MENU TO DESELECT THE CRAB. AND USE THE PAINTBRUSH TOOL (WITH DIFFERENT FADE-OUT RATES) TO BLEND THE EDGES INTO THE BACKGROUND.

4 Choose Lighten from the Mode pop-up menu.

The Lighten mode affects only pixels that are darker than the beginning color.

5 Starting in a light color, smudge outward into the darker area.

Only the darker pixels are changed.

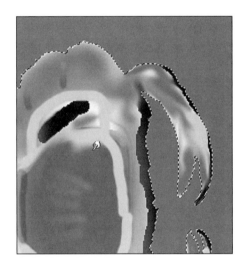

Undoing all your changes

Since smudging using the painting modes can produce some unusual and unique effects, you may not be happy with your first attempts at using the Lighten and Darken modes. As you already know, you can undo your last action using the Undo command. Adobe Photoshop also provides a quick way to return to your last-saved version of a file when you want to undo all the changes you've made.

To retrieve the last-saved version of a file:

1 Choose Revert from the File menu. A dialog box appears asking you to confirm your choice.

2 Click OK.

The saved version of the file retains any selections you saved in the original file. However, when you revert to a file, it opens without any current selection.

3 Choose Load Selection from the Select menu and #5 from the submenu to continue working with the crab selection.

4 Try using the smudge tool with the painting modes again.

5 Continue experimenting with the smudge tool (and any of the other tools) until you're satisfied with your image. It should look something like the following illustration.

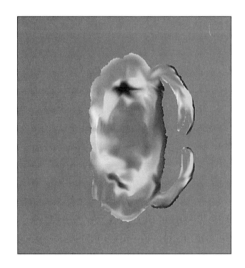

6 Save the file as PAINTED3.PSD.

CROPPING AN IMAGE

Now that you've finished painting the crab, you're going to add another element to this image. As part of the design of the final cookbook cover, you want to copy the lemon slice from your original CRAB.PSD file into the PAINTED3.PSD file.

 To make the copying easier, you're going to crop the section of the image you want to copy using the *cropping tool.*

To crop the image:

1 Open the CRAB.PSD file from LESSON1.

2 Click the cropping tool in the toolbox and move the pointer into the image area. Notice that the pointer turns into a cropping icon.

Place the pointer to the left and slightly above the bottom lemon slice.

3 Drag down and to the right to select the lemon slice.

It doesn't matter if you include part of the plate and the parsley in the area. You just want to include the entire lemon slice in the crop. If you want to change the size of the cropped area, position the pointer on one of the corner square boxes and drag. Choose Undo and try again if the selection border doesn't include all of the lemon.

4 Move the pointer outside the cropped selection. The pointer appears as the international symbol for "No," indicating that clicking in this area cancels the cropping action.

5 Move the pointer inside the cropping selection. The pointer turns into a pair of scissors, meaning that clicking in this area confirms the cropping.

6 Click with the scissors pointer.

The cropped image appears in a resized window. In addition to changing what you see, cropping an image also reduces its file size. Working with smaller files is one way to improve Adobe Photoshop's performance.

COPYING A SELECTION FROM ONE FILE TO ANOTHER

Because Adobe Photoshop lets you have several documents open at one time, it's easy to copy a selection from one file to another, or to sample colors from one image to use in another image.

To copy the lemon slice:

1 Double-click the elliptical marquee tool in the toolbox. The Elliptical Marquee Options dialog box appears.

You can soften the effect of a pasted selection by smoothing the selection's hard edges. *Feathering* a selection blurs the edges by building a gradual transition boundary between the selection and the surrounding pixels. The Feather Radius option in the elliptical and rectangular marquee tool dialog boxes specifies how far inside *and* outside the selection border the feathering extends. For more information on feathering, see the *Adobe Photoshop User Guide.*

2 Enter 2 in the Feather Radius text box, and click OK.

3 Choose Zoom In from the Window menu.

4 Position the crosshair in the center of the lemon slice. Hold down the Alt key as you drag to start the marquee from the center.

If your selection is the right size but in the wrong place, hold down the Control and Alt keys as you drag the selection border (you will see the arrow pointer when you're directly over the selection border). This Control+Alt drag shortcut works any time you want to reposition a selection border.

5 Choose Copy from the Edit menu. The lemon selection is copied to the Clipboard.

6 Click the PAINTED3.PSD window to make it active, or choose Painted 3 from the bottom of the Window menu.

7 Choose Paste from the Edit menu.

The lemon appears in the center of the PAINTED3.PSD file.

When selections are pasted, they are *floating selections.* This means they can be moved without affecting the underlying pixels. (Once a selection is *defloated*, moving it reveals the background color in its former location.) See the *Adobe Photoshop User Guide* for more information on floating and defloating selections.

8 Drag the lemon until it is in the lower-left corner of the crab.

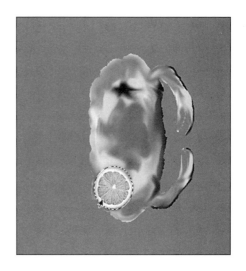

9 Save the file in your Projects directory as PAINTED4.PSD.

10 Choose Crab from the bottom of the Window menu to return to the CRAB.PSD image.

11 Click the close box in the upper-left corner of the title bar to close the CRAB.PSD file. Do not save the changes to the CRAB.PSD file.

USING THE RUBBER STAMP TOOL

Now that the lemon is pasted into the image, you're going to duplicate (or clone) it using the *rubber stamp tool.* The rubber stamp tool samples, or picks up, an area of the image, then duplicates that area as you paint.

To clone the lemon:

1 Choose None from the Select menu to deselect the lemon slice.

Remember, if there is an active selection in an area, the painting tools work only in the selected area.

2 Click the rubber stamp tool in the toolbox and move into the image area. Notice that the pointer becomes a rubber stamp.

Cloning, or exact duplication of the sampled area, is the default setting for the rubber stamp tool.

3 Alt+click the rubber stamp in the upper-left corner of the lemon slice to set the sampling point.

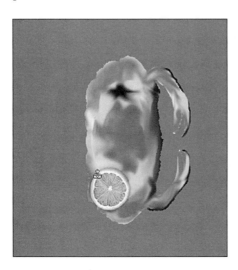

The *sampling point* is the starting point of the area you want to duplicate.

4 Position the pointer above, and slightly to the right of, the top of the crab, hold down the mouse button, and begin tracing the outline of the lemon slice.

As you paint, a crosshair appears, showing you the part of the original sample that's being applied.

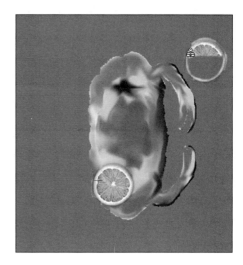

Move slowly and watch your sampling point. Don't worry if you include part of the crab shell; you'll learn how to correct this in a minute. If you want to start over, choose Undo from the Edit menu.

Painting with an aligned sampling point

By default, the rubber stamp tool paints with the aligned Clone option. This means that Adobe Photoshop remembers how far the sampling point is from the location where you began painting. For example, in the lemon slice you just painted, the sampling point is about 2-1/2 inches down and 2 inches to the left of the painting point.

If you move the rubber stamp pointer and begin painting again, the distance between the sampling point and the painting point will be the same (that is, the sampling point will be 2-1/2 inches down and 2 inches to the left of where you're painting). Each time you stop and then resume painting, the sampling point moves to maintain this distance.

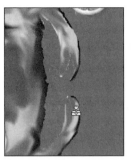

Sampling point

Painting with aligned Clone option

If this seems confusing, move the rubber stamp down and over the crab claw and start painting again. You will see that you're painting with the red background, which is the location of the new sampling point.

Painting with a non-aligned sampling point

The non-aligned Clone option applies a sampled image from the same initial sampling point, no matter how many times you stop and resume painting.

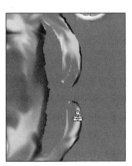
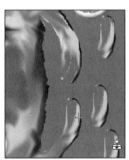

Sampling point

Painting with non-aligned Clone option

To paint with a non-aligned sampling point:

1 Double-click the rubber stamp tool. The Rubber Stamp Options dialog box appears.

2 Choose Clone (non-aligned) from the Option pop-up menu.

3 If you changed it, reset the sampling point at the top left of the far-left lemon.

4 Paint a lemon in the upper-left and lower-right corners of the crab.

No matter where you place the rubber stamp, you always begin painting from the same sampling point.

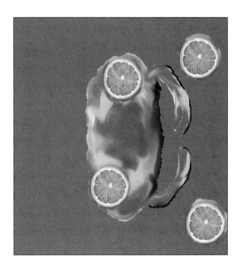

Painting from a saved version of the file

You can also use the rubber stamp tool to clone areas from the last-saved version of the file. This is useful for cleaning up areas around a cloned section. You'll use this option now to remove any parts of the crab shell that might have been cloned with your lemon slices.

TIP: TO SET THE
OPPOSITE COLOR FROM
THE OUTLINED COLOR
SELECTION BOX, HOLD
DOWN THE ALT KEY AND
CLICK THE EYEDROPPER.
FOR EXAMPLE, IF THE
FOREGROUND COLOR
SELECTION BOX IS OUT-
LINED, HOLD DOWN
THE ALT KEY TO SET A
NEW BACKGROUND
COLOR.

Using this option allows you to *selectively revert* part of the image. The effect is like painting with the magic eraser option for the eraser tool. The advantage of using the rubber stamp tool, however, is that you can choose a brush size to paint with (the eraser limits you to painting using the rectangular eraser pointer).

To clone areas from a saved version of the file:

1 In the Rubber Stamp Options dialog box, choose From Saved in the Option pop-up menu.

2 Zoom in so you can position the rubber stamp tool in an area where the background has been cloned with the lemon slice. (This procedure won't work with the lemon slice you copied from the *Crab* image, only with those you have cloned in this image.)

3 Choose a narrow brush from the Brushes palette.

4 Begin painting around the lemon.

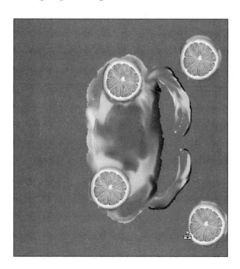

The red background replaces the inadvertently cloned areas.

You can also use the rubber stamp tool to paint with a pattern or an impressionistic effect. See the *Adobe Photoshop User Guide* for more information on these options.

5 Return to the 1:1 view ratio.

6 Save this new image as PAINTED5.PSD.

SELECTING WITH A FIXED MARQUEE

Although the lemons look like they're floating in space, their placement will add cohesiveness to the final design. To make the image more attractive, you're going to eliminate some of the unneeded areas using the Crop command.

When you used the cropping tool, you dragged to indicate the marquee for the section you wanted to crop. This worked fine, since you didn't need to be very precise in the area you selected.

In cropping the area for the final book cover, you want to match the exact dimensions needed for the final art. To do this, you're going to use a *fixed marquee* to select the area to be cropped with the Crop command.

To specify a fixed marquee:

1 Double-click the rectangular marquee tool in the toolbox. The Rectangular Marquee Options dialog box appears.

2 Under Fixed Size, enter 185 for the Width and 290 for the Height, then click OK.

3 Click anywhere in the image to make the fixed marquee appear.

4 Hold down the Control and Alt keys and drag the marquee until its left edge is about 2-1/8 inches from the left edge of the window and its top is about 1 inch from the top of the window.

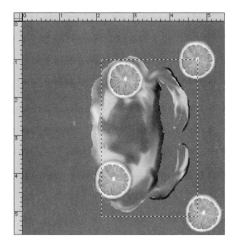

5 Choose Crop from the Edit menu.

The cropped image appears in a resized window.

6 Save this image as PAINTED6.PSD.

You can also set a rectangular marquee to have a specific height-to-width ratio, or to select a single row or column. (The elliptical marquee tool can also use a fixed-size or constrained-ratio setting.) See the *Adobe Photoshop User Guide* for more information on these options.

CHANGING THE CANVAS SIZE

Up to now, your image has taken up the entire window. Now you're going to add space to the image while keeping all of your cropped crab (and without changing the image dimensions of the image). To add space, you increase the *canvas size.* The canvas area appears in the background color.

To add extra canvas area:

1 Click the eyedropper tool in the toolbox.

2 Make sure the background color selection box is outlined in the Colors palette.

3 Click to sample a dark blue-gray color from the image for the new background color (or you can sample the color from the final image).

If the foreground color changed, you probably didn't have the background color selection box outlined.

4 Choose Canvas Size from the Image menu. The Canvas Size dialog box appears.

5 Make sure the unit measurement pop-up menu is set to inches, then add about three-quarters of an inch to the width of the image by entering 3.333 in the Width text box.

6 Click the middle-right square in the Placement box to indicate where you want to position the image in the new canvas area.

7 Click OK.

The image should look like this:

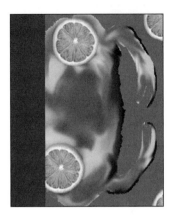

OPENING AN EPS FILE

At the end of Lesson 1, you learned how to fill a selection with the foreground color. You can also fill a selection using a pattern. Several patterns are included in your Adobe Photoshop software. One of these patterns, INTSUR.PSD, has been copied to your LESSON2 directory.

To open an EPS file:

1 Choose Open from the File menu and select the INTSUR.EPS file in the LESSON2 directory.

The EPS Rasterizer dialog box appears.

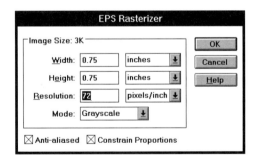

The Adobe Photoshop patterns are all in Encapsulated PostScript file (EPS) format. The EPS format is used by many illustration and page-layout applications. When you open an EPS file in Adobe Photoshop, the image is *rasterized*—that is, the mathematically defined lines and curves of the *vector* image are converted to the points (or pixels) displayed in Adobe Photoshop. See the *Adobe Photoshop User Guide* for more information on using EPS files.

2 Click OK to accept the default settings.

Since this is a grayscale file, your screen may temporarily turn black and white while this window is active. Don't worry, the color will return when you select another window.

FILLING WITH A PATTERN

Filling with a pattern consists of two steps: first you define the pattern which stores it in the *pattern buffer* (similar to a Clipboard for patterns), then you fill using this stored pattern. *There can only be one defined pattern at a time.* When you next define a pattern, it replaces the current pattern in the pattern buffer.

To define a pattern:

1 Choose All from the Select menu (or press Control+A).

This selects the entire contents of the INTSUR.EPS file.

2 Choose Define Pattern from the Edit menu.

The pattern is copied to the pattern buffer.

3 Close the INTSUR.EPS window.

4 Double-click the rectangular marquee tool and change the marquee setting back to Normal.

5 Select the blue area in the PAINTED6.PSD image.

6 Choose Fill from the Edit menu.

7 Select the Pattern option, make sure the Opacity is set to 100 percent, and choose the Darken option from the Mode menu.

The opacity and mode options in the Fill dialog box produce the same effect as changing the opacity and mode settings on the Brushes palette for a tool. The Darken option fills only pixels that are lighter than the fill color.

8 Click OK to fill the selection.

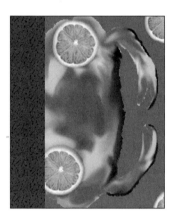

PREVIEWING THE IMAGE SIZE

To add a little interest to the plain canvas area, you're going to create a thin gradient fill along the right edge of the solid color area. In order to select the area for the gradient fill, you will again use a fixed marquee.

Since you want the gradient to extend in a narrow strip from the top to the bottom of the window, you want this fixed marquee to be exactly as high as the image. You can determine the height of an image by using the page preview box.

To display the size preview information:

1 Position the pointer on the page preview box in the lower-left corner of the window (this box currently shows you the file size).

2 Hold down the Alt key and mouse button. The size preview box appears.

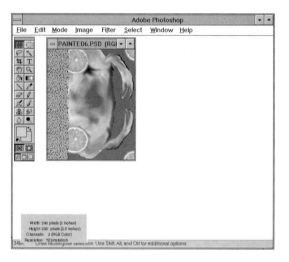

If what you see looks like a rectangle with diagonal lines, you're looking at the placement of the image on the printed page. (You'll use this feature in Lesson 11.) You must hold down the Alt key when you click this box to see the size preview box.

In addition to the height, this box also shows you the width, resolution, and number of channels in the image. Note that the image is 290 pixels high.

CREATING A GRADIENT FILL

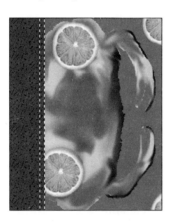 A gradient fill displays a gradual transition from the foreground color to the background color. You use the *gradient tool* to create a gradient fill.

A *linear* gradient fill creates a gradient from one point to another in a straight line (you can create *radial* gradient fills, too). The gradient begins at the point where you start to drag and ends at the point where you release the mouse. You will use a fixed marquee to select the area for a linear gradient fill.

To create the gradient fill:

1 In the Rectangular Marquee Options dialog box, select the Fixed Size option and enter 8 for the Width and 290 for the Height, then click OK.

2 Click near the right edge of the blue area to display the marquee, then hold down the Control and Alt keys to drag the marquee until it is along the right edge of the canvas.

3 Make sure the foreground color selection box is outlined, then select the white in the top row of the Colors palette as the new foreground color (the blue-gray you sampled when you created the canvas should still be the background color).

4 Choose the gradient tool from the toolbox.

5 Hold down the Shift key to keep the line straight as you draw, then drag from the top to the bottom of the selected area.

 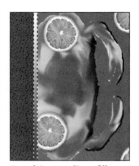

Drag from top to bottom   *Resulting gradient fill*

The gradient fills the selected area starting with white (the foreground color) at the top and ending with blue-gray (the background color) at the bottom.

6 Set the marquee back to the Normal option in the Rectangular Marquee Options dialog box.

7 Click anywhere outside the selection.

When there is an active selection, clicking in the image has the same effect as choosing None from the Select menu—whatever was selected is deselected.

8 Save the file as PAINTED7.PSD.

ADDING TYPE TO THE IMAGE

The final phase of producing your cookbook cover is to add words to the image. You will use the *type tool* to enter the type.

To add type to the image:

1 Click the type tool in the toolbox, then click a starting location for the type at the left edge of the crab (you're going to add the bottom word first).

The Type Tool dialog box appears.

2 Choose Helvetica from the Font menu and select Bold under Style.

3 Type 42 in the Size text box.

4 Type **Classics** in the text box at the bottom of the dialog box.

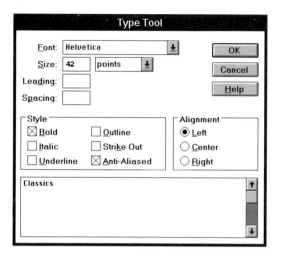

5 Click OK.

When you create type it appears as a floating selection. As long as it is floating, you can move it anywhere in the image.

6 Drag the type to position it so that the **s** at the end of **Classics** is between the two claws.

You can move the selection in pixel increments by pressing the arrow keys.

7 Click outside the type to deselect it.

8 With the type tool selected, click the canvas area to add the rest of the type. Type **Creole** in the text box, and click OK.

9 Position the first line of type as shown in the CBOOK.PSD file.

10 Deselect the type and save the file.

11 Close both files.

And, there you are! In only two lessons, you've come a long way. Just compare this final image with the crab-on-plate you started with to gauge exactly how much you've learned.

SAVING THE PALETTES

During the course of this lesson, you learned how to customize both the Brushes palette and the Colors palette. These same palettes, with the new colors and brushes, will appear the next time you open Adobe Photoshop.

As you become more familiar with Adobe Photoshop, you will probably find yourself using customized palettes more and more. As you add colors and brushes, you may want to save individual palettes to use with specific projects. (For example, Adobe Photoshop provides some color palettes to use with specific custom inks.)

To save your palettes:

1 Choose Save Brushes from the Brushes palette Control menu.

2 Open your Projects directory, type NEW-BRUSH.ABR (extension) to name the palette, and click OK.

When you're doing your own work, you might want to save this palette in the Adobe Photoshop Brushes and Palettes directory along with the other palettes.

3 Choose Save Colors from the Colors palette Control menu.

4 Type NEWCOLOR.ACO (extension) to name the palette and save the file in your Projects directory.

To switch between palettes, you use the Load Brushes and Load Colors commands in the palette Control menus. To return to the original palettes, select the *Default Brushes* and *Default Colors* palettes in the Brushes and Palettes directory.

With the knowledge you've gained in these first two lessons, you're well on your way to becoming an experienced Adobe Photoshop user. In the next lesson, you'll review what you've learned and put your skills to use by editing another culinary creation.

LE MONDE

B

Gourmet Visions

Lesson

3

Lesson 3: Review Project— Advertisement

This lesson gives you a chance to practice the commands and techniques you learned in the first two lessons of *Classroom in a Book*. Nothing new is introduced in this lesson (although you will learn some alternative ways to perform tasks you're already familiar with). You'll probably be amazed at how dramatically you can transform an image using the knowledge and experience you already have.

This lesson provides step-by-step instructions that you can follow at your own pace. If you find that you can't remember how to do something, or need to remind yourself of a shortcut, refer back to Lessons 1 and 2. It should take you about 45 minutes to complete this lesson.

In Lesson 2, most of your efforts were directed toward *painting* the crab and producing an artistic version of the image. In this lesson, you'll use many of the same tools and commands to *edit* an image. You'll start with an attractive, if rather traditional, image of crawdads. You'll end up with a crisper, flashier version of the same subject as it might appear in a seafood advertisement.

Source file (CRAW.PSD) *Ending image (CRAWDAD.PSD)*

Especially in this lesson, feel free to try out different colors and settings as you edit the image. Use the ending image as a guide, but don't feel restricted to reproducing an exact replica.

BEGINNING THIS LESSON

Again, in this lesson, you will have two images open on the screen: the file you begin with and the final version of the image.

To begin this lesson:

1 Open the CRAW.PSD file in the LESSON3 directory and choose Show Rulers from the Window menu to turn on the rulers in this file.

2 Open the CRAWDAD.PSD file in the LESSON3 directory as your reference file.

3 Zoom out to reduce the CRAWDAD.PSD image, resize the window, then drag the window to the upper-right corner of your screen.

4 Be sure the Brushes and Colors palettes are open. You can collapse the palettes if you want to.

MAKING A COMPLEX SELECTION

The first thing you're going to do to edit this image is select the plate.

To make the selection:

1 Activate the CRAW.PSD window.

2 Zoom in to expand the CRAWDAD.PSD image.

3 Set the tolerance in the Magic Wand Options dialog box to 32.

TIP: HOLD DOWN
THE SHIFT KEY AND USE
THE ELLIPTICAL MAR-
QUEE TOOL TO SELECT
THE UPPER GLASS,
THEN MAKE FINE
CORRECTIONS WITH
THE LASSO TOOL.

4 Position the wand under the bottle in the upper-right corner of the plate so that the wand is about 1-1/2 inches from the top of the window and 3 inches from the left edge, then click.

This selects a large portion of the plate; however, you will have to use other selection tools and commands to select the entire plate.

5 Choose Similar from the Select menu.

Notice that the selection now includes the area between the crawdads. The Similar command, you might remember, selects pixels of similar color anywhere in an image, whereas the Grow command selects *adjacent* pixels within the tolerance level.

Unfortunately, the selection also includes a lot of areas that you don't need. You'll delete these areas in a minute.

6 Choose Grow from the Select menu.

This increases the selection so that all the gray areas around and between the crawdads are included in the selection.

7 Use the lasso tool with the Control key to subtract the unneeded areas outside of the plate.

Draw a rough approximation of the outside of the plate where the bottle covers it. The glasses and the crawdads should not be in the selection.

8 Zoom in and use the lasso tool with the Shift key to add areas to the selection. Make sure the part of the flower that is on the plate is included in the selection.

When you're finished, your selection should look like the following illustration.

9 Choose Save Selection from the Select menu to save the selection in a channel.

10 Save the file as CRAW1.PSD in your Projects directory.

FILLING THE SELECTION

In the final image, you want the plate to have a flat, untextured tone. To accomplish this, you're going to fill the selection by sampling a color from the plate.

To fill the selection:

1 Use the eyedropper to sample the plate above the flower.

2 Choose Fill from the Edit menu, click Foreground Color, set the Opacity to 95percent, choose Luminosity from the Mode pop-up menu, and then click OK.

The Luminosity mode changes the brightness of the pixels; the hue and saturation are not affected. Notice how the appearance of the flower changes. The flower is less bright, but its color remains brown.

The fill has left a slight green tone in the area where the bottle used to overlap the plate. To complete the fill, you need to subtly blend this area into the surrounding pixels.

3 Set the Distance in the Airbrush Options dialog box to 0.

4 Zoom in and use the airbrush with a medium brush to cover the green tint. You may need to sample a gray near the top of the plate to get the correct color.

SAVING MULTIPLE SELECTIONS

Later in this lesson, when you create a shadow around the plate, you will need the plate (and everything on it) included in the selection. You're going to create and save this selection before you begin working on the image background.

To save the second selection:

1 Use the lasso to add the crawdads and the glasses to the selection.

2 Choose Save Selection from the Select menu and New from the submenu.

The selection is saved in channel #5. If you had chosen the #4 channel, this selection would have overwritten the first selection you saved.

3 Deselect the selection.

4 Save the file as CRAW2.PSD.

TIP: YOU CAN HOLD
DOWN THE SHIFT KEY
AND CLICK IN EACH
CORNER OF THE SELEC-
TION TO PAINT IN A
STRAIGHT LINE FROM
POINT TO POINT.

DEFINING THE BACKGROUND PATTERN

In Lesson 2, you filled a path with a pattern supplied with the Adobe Photoshop software. Now you're going to create a pattern from elements in this image. The pattern you're going to use consists of a series of square tiles.

To create the pattern:

1 Zoom in on the lower-right corner of the image.

2 Double-click the rectangular marquee tool and set the marquee to Normal.

3 Position the crosshair about 3-1/2 inches from the left edge of the window and 4-3/4 inches from the top of the window.

4 Hold down the Shift key to constrain the selection to a square, then drag to create about a 1-1/8-inch square selection (the bottom edge of the selection will extend below the board).

To make the pattern "tile" large enough, you need to remove the table from the bottom part of the selection.

5 Use the rubber stamp tool with the Clone (aligned) option and Alt-click to sample the blue board.

6 Paint the bottom of the selection.

Now you need to add the border around the edge of the tile.

7 Scroll up and use the eyedropper to sample the dark green of the bottle as the foreground color.

8 Use the paintbrush tool with a fine brush and an Opacity setting of 70 percent to paint along the edges of the tile selection. Hold down the Shift key as you paint to stroke in a straight line.

9 Choose a slightly harder brush and paint along the bottom edge twice more to add depth to the tile.

10 Choose Define Pattern from the Edit menu.

This stores the pattern in the pattern buffer.

DELETING CANVAS FROM THE IMAGE

Right now, the plate is off-center. You're going to center the plate before you fill it with the pattern by deleting some of the bottom and left side of the image.

To delete some canvas:

1 Return to the 1:1 view of the image.

2 Choose Canvas Size from the Image menu and enter a Width of 4.3 inches and a Height of 5.5 inches in the dialog box.

3 Click the upper-right square in the Placement box to delete canvas from the bottom and left side of the image, then click OK.

4 Since you do want to reduce the size of the canvas, click Proceed when you see the warning box.

The extra space is removed and the plate appears in the center of the image.

FILLING WITH A PATTERN

Now you're ready to replace the area surrounding the plate with the new background.

To fill the background:

1 Choose Load Selection from the Select menu and #5 from the submenu.

The selection that includes all of the plate appears.

2 Choose Inverse from the Select menu so that the area around the plate is selected.

3 Fill the selection using the Pattern option, 100 percent Opacity, and the Normal mode.

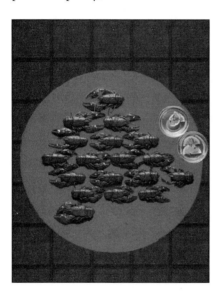

4 Save the file.

CREATING A SHADOW EFFECT

As the final element in the background, you're going to add a shadow at the bottom of the plate.

To create a shadow:

1 Choose Inverse from the Select menu to return to a selection that includes the plate.

2 Choose Copy from the Edit menu to put a copy of the selection on the Clipboard.

You will need to paste this selection over the shadow you create. Note that when you *save* a selection, you save the shape or outline of the selection (the selection border). When you *copy* a selection, you keep the contents of the selected area.

3 Click a selection tool, hold down the Control and Alt keys, and drag the selection border down and slightly to the left.

4 Choose Feather from the Select menu and enter a feather radius of 5.

Note that to feather a selection *as you draw* the selection border, you use the Feather Radius option in the Rectangular or Elliptical Marquee Options dialog boxes (as you did with the elliptical marquee tool in Lesson 2). To feather a selection *after the border is drawn*, you use the Feather command.

5 Click the default colors icon to make black the foreground color.

6 Hold down the Alt key as you press Delete.

The selection is filled with black. Pressing Alt-Delete is equivalent to using the Fill command with the foreground color, 100 percent opacity, and Normal mode options.

7 Choose Load Selection from the Select menu and #5 from the submenu.

Loading the selection returns the selection border to its original location.

8 Choose Paste from the Edit menu to see the shadow effect.

9 Deselect the selection and save the file as CRAW3.PSD.

CLONING PART OF THE IMAGE

To change the visual balance of the crawdads, you're going to add one more crawdad in the upper-right corner of the plate. To do this, you will again use the rubber stamp tool.

To clone a crawdad:

1 Zoom in on the top three rows of crawdads.

2 Make sure the Clone (non-aligned) option is set in the Rubber Stamp Options dialog box, then Alt-click to set the sampling point on the center crawdad in the third row.

3 Choose the far-left brush in the second row of the Brushes palette and set the Opacity to 100 percent.

4 Move the rubber stamp to the right of the top crawdad and begin painting.

5 Continue painting until you have duplicated the crawdad.

If you run out of room, choose Undo and try again.

6 If necessary, use the From Saved option with the rubber stamp tool to touch up the area around the edges of the crawdad. When you've finished, the image should look something like this.

7 Save the image as CRAW4.PSD.

CREATING TYPE WITH A DROP SHADOW

As a final touch to this advertisement, you're going to add type to this image and then put a drop shadow around the type. This drop shadow will complement the shadow you created under the plate.

To add the type:

1 Make sure the foreground color is black and the background color is white.

2 Click the type tool and then click the insertion point about three-quarters of an inch down and one-quarter of an inch in from the left edge of the window.

3 In the Type Tool dialog box, choose Times from the Font menu, set the size to 48 points, and type **Dad's Delight** in the text box, then click OK to display the type.

4 Drag or use the arrow keys to center the type above the plate.

The black type is the drop shadow. Now you're ready to add the white type.

5 Copy the floating type to the Clipboard, then paste a copy of the type back into the image.

6 Click the switch colors icon to make white the foreground color.

7 Fill the type with the foreground color by setting the Opacity to 100 percent and using the Normal mode.

8 Use the arrow keys to move the type two pixels up and two pixels to the right, then deselect the type to see the final image.

9 Save the file, then close both files.

Give yourself a pat on the back! In a short time, you have completely changed the look and feel of the crawdad image. With this experience behind you, you're ready to explore some of the more advanced aspects of Adobe Photoshop in Lessons 4 and 5.

LE MONDE

B

Gourmet Visions

PATHS, MASKS AND CHANNELS

Lesson 4: Paths, Masks, and Channels

This lesson builds on your knowledge of using selections as masks, and expands on the concept of channels that was introduced when you first saved selections. It also introduces a new tool that allows you to draw paths you can convert into selections.

In this lesson, you'll begin with a new, empty file. Using some new as well as some familiar tools, you'll draw in the new file, copy a selection from a photograph into this file, and then manipulate the selection to create a final, almost cartoon-like image. It should take you about 60 to 90 minutes to complete this lesson.

In this lesson, you'll learn how to do the following:

- open a new file

- use the pen tool to draw paths

- change a path into a selection

- use the Quick Mask mode

- save, name, and view a channel

- paste one selection behind another

- posterize an image

- stroke a path

At the end of this lesson, you'll have an eye-catching display sign for red peppers, sure to attract the attention of Gourmet Visions, produce customers.

The following images show the photograph you'll borrow from and the final image.

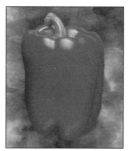 

Source file   *Ending image*
(RPEPPER.PSD)   *(PPOSTER.PSD)*

BEGINNING THIS LESSON

In previous lessons, you've begun with an existing Adobe Photoshop image and modified it. In this lesson, you'll create a new file starting with a blank window. Because you're starting from scratch, you'll probably find it especially helpful to refer to the final image as you work through this lesson.

To begin this lesson:

1 Open the PPOSTER.PSD file in the LESSON4 directory.

2 Zoom out to reduce the image, resize the window, then drag the window to the upper-right corner of your screen.

3 Choose Show Rulers from the Window menu to turn on the rulers in the reference file.

4 Collapse the Brushes and Colors palettes and move them to the bottom of your screen so you have more working room. You can close or hide any other palettes.

OPENING A NEW FILE

Now you're ready to open a new, empty Adobe Photoshop file.

To open a new file:

1 Choose New from the File menu (or press Control+N). The new dialog box appears so you can set the size for the new file.

2 If necessary, choose inches from the pop-up menus, then enter 6 inches in the Width box and 5 inches in the Height box. The other two options should be left at their default values—Resolution at 72 and Mode at RGB Color.

3 Click OK to create the file.

An empty, untitled window appears.

4 Turn on the rulers and save this file in your Projects directory as SIGN1.PSD.

USING THE PEN TOOL

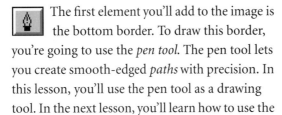 The first element you'll add to the image is the bottom border. To draw this border, you're going to use the *pen tool.* The pen tool lets you create smooth-edged *paths* with precision. In this lesson, you'll use the pen tool as a drawing tool. In the next lesson, you'll learn how to use the pen tool as a selection tool.

To draw a straight line path:

1 Choose Show Paths from the Window menu. The Paths palette appears.

The five tools across the top of the palette are used to create and edit paths. When you save a path, its name appears in the scroll box below the tools.

2 Drag the Paths palette to the right so that it is below the reference image.

3 Click the pen tool (the second tool from the left) in the Paths palette.

4 Move the pointer to the lower-left corner of the SIGN1.PSD window and click.

The solid square that appears is a smooth *anchor point.* This point is selected until you click the next point.

5 Move the pointer up and to the right until the ruler markers are at about three-quarters of an inch from the left edge and about 4 inches from the top edge, then click again.

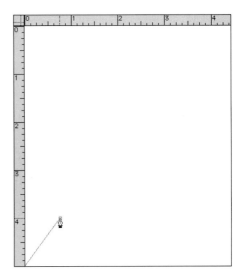

The second anchor point is selected, and the first anchor point changes to a hollow square. A line connects the two anchor points.

6 Move the pointer until it's near the bottom of the window and slightly beyond the 1-1/2-inch mark, then click.

Don't worry about the exact location; you'll learn how to edit the points in a minute. If your line has curves and additional lines coming out of it, you're probably dragging instead of clicking. You must *click* to draw straight lines with the pen tool.

You can use Undo to remove the last anchor point, or press Backspace twice to erase the entire path if you want to start over.

7 Continue clicking until you've drawn the bottom border (there are five triangles in the border). Your last click should be in the bottom-right corner of the window.

Use the rulers in the final image as a guide for placing your points.

8 To close the path, move the pen tool from the last point outside the bottom of the window, and click the first anchor point again.

A small loop appears next to the pointer when you place it on the first anchor point. This loop tells you that the next click closes the path.

EDITING A STRAIGHT PATH

When the anchor points in a path are visible, that path is selected. Using the tools in the Paths palette, you can adjust the anchor points to change the shape of a selected path.

To edit the straight path:

1 Click the arrow pointer at the far left of the Paths palette.

2 Drag an anchor point to change its location.

If the anchor points aren't visible, click anywhere on the path to display them. Experiment with moving the anchor points until you have the border you want.

3 If the line along the bottom of the path is not quite at the window's bottom edge, drag the bottom right and left points down. You don't want any space between the bottom of the path and the bottom of the window.

SAVING A PATH

Just as it's a good idea to save selections in case you want to reuse them, it's also a good idea to save paths that you might want to use again in the image.

To save a path:

1 Choose Save Path from the Paths palette pop-up menu. The Save Path dialog box appears.

2 Name the path *Border* and click OK.

The path is listed in the Paths palette. The check mark before the path means that it's selected. In order for this path to be a permanent part of this file, you must also save the file.

3 Save the file as SIGN2.PSD.

ADDING TO THE PATH

Now you're ready to add the top border. Although you can have multiple paths in a file, only one path is visible at a time. Once a path is saved and is the selected path, any additions, deletions, or editing changes you make are saved under that path name. This means that as you draw the top border, it becomes part of the *Border* path.

The top border consists of both straight segments and curved segments. First you'll set the anchor points for the straight segments.

To begin the top border:

1 Click the pen tool in the Paths palette.

2 Click the top-right corner of the window to begin adding to the path.

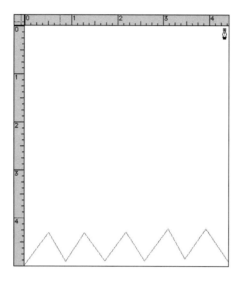

3 Click the top-left corner to make the first straight segment run across the top of the window.

4 Move the pointer down along the left edge of the window to about the 2-1/2-inch marker, and click once more.

DRAWING A CURVED PATH SEGMENT

Drawing a curved segment is slightly different from drawing a straight segment. When you draw a straight path with the pen tool, you *click* to set the anchor points. When you draw a curve with the pen tool, you *drag* in the direction you want the curve to be drawn.

To draw a curve:

1 Move the pointer so that it is about 1-1/4 inches from the top and about 2-1/2 inches from the left edge of the window.

2 Drag the pointer up and to the right.

As you drag, a *direction line* appears. The two *direction points* at either end of the line move in opposition to each other around the anchor point. The length and slope of the direction line determines the length and slope of the curve.

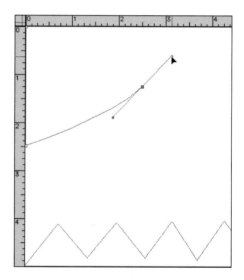

3 Position the pen so that it's about 5-1/4 inches from the left edge of the window and about three-eighths of an inch from the top, then drag a short distance to the right to set another point.

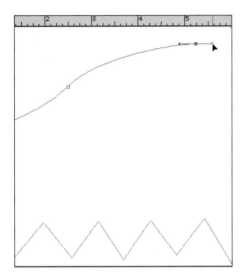

4 Move the pointer slightly down and to the right edge of the window, then click to add a straight segment to the path.

5 Close the path by clicking the first anchor point in the upper-right corner of the window.

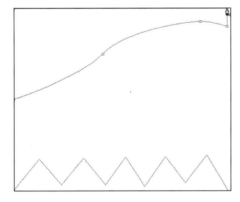

6 Click the arrow pointer in the Paths palette and click an anchor point to make the direction line reappear.

7 Drag the direction points to adjust the slope of the curve until it looks similar to the path shown below.

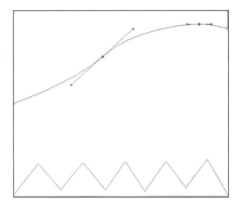

Notice that the slope of the direction line for the first anchor point is rather steep; the slope of the direction line for the second anchor point is flatter.

Only the top part of the path is currently selected. This is because the path consists of two *subpaths*.

8 Click anywhere in the window outside the paths to deselect the top subpath.

You don't have to save again because the new part of the path is automatically saved as part of the *Border* path. To see that both borders are part of the *Border* path, you're going to deselect the path and then make it visible again.

9 Click anywhere in the gray area of the Paths palette (don't click the path name).

The path disappears from the SIGN2.PSD window and the check mark before the *Border* name in the Paths palette is removed.

10 Click *Border* in the Paths palette.

The path (with both subpaths included) appears in the window.

FILLING THE PATH

Paths, like selections, can be filled with the foreground color or a pattern. To fill this path, you're going to learn a new way to create a custom color.

To fill the path:

1 Uncollapse the Colors palette.

2 Make sure the foreground color selection box in the Colors palette is outlined.

3 Click the medium blue swatch in the second row of the Colors palette (the tenth swatch from the right).

Although you might think of this color as *blue*, it actually consists of a mix of the three primary colors—red, green, and blue (often abbreviated as *RGB*). The numbers to the right of the sliders in the Colors palette show the values for each component, about 76 for the red (R) value, 106 for the green (G) value, and 164 for the blue (B) value. (The numbers in your palette might be different, depending on your hardware and calibration. The beginning numbers don't matter for this example.)

4 Drag the red slider to the left until it reads about 20, drag the green slider to the left until it reads about 15, and drag the blue slider to the left until it reads about 74.

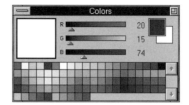

As you move the sliders, the color in the foreground color selection box changes to reflect the new values. Don't worry about selecting exactly the same values. The resulting color should be a deep, rich blue.

5 Choose Fill Path from the Paths palette pop-up menu. The Fill Path dialog box appears.

6 Make sure that Foreground Color is selected, the Opacity is set to 100 percent, and the mode is Normal, then click OK.

The path is filled with your custom foreground color. If you like this color, you might want to add it to the Colors palette before continuing with the lesson.

7 Save the file as SIGN3.PSD.

WORKING WITH MASKS

 Now you're ready to add the peppers to the image. To do this, you're going to select the pepper while working in the *Quick Mask mode.*

 To leave the Quick Mask mode, you click the Standard mode control.

You create and use a *mask* when you want to isolate part of an image to copy it, apply color changes, or apply special effects (or to prevent these actions from applying to an area in the image). The Quick Mask mode is useful for making these selections because it lets you see the masks and the image at the same time. You can then edit the mask using the painting and editing tools.

To create the mask:

1 Open the RPEPPER.PSD file in the LESSON4 directory.

2 Click the magic wand anywhere in the area outside of the pepper.

Because of its irregular shape, you're going to select the background and then inverse the selection to end up with a selected pepper. This is easier than using the selection tools to isolate the complex outline of the pepper itself.

3 Choose Grow from the Select menu once or twice, until most of the background is selected. Leave some areas unselected.

4 Click the Quick Mask mode control in the toolbox.

By default, the mask appears in red and has an opacity of 50 percent—similar to a rubylith overlay, or *frisket,* used in traditional illustration masking. Everything that appears in red, including the parts of the background that were not selected, would be masked (protected from change) if you applied a fill or a special effect. Because the pepper that you're trying to select is also red, a red mask is not very helpful in this instance.

5 Double-click the Quick Mask mode control. The Mask Options dialog box appears.

6 Click the color swatch in the dialog box to display the Color Picker.

7 Move the slider up until green appears in the color field, then click a bright green color in the color field.

8 Click OK to close the Color Picker and return to the Mask Options dialog box.

9 Set the Opacity to 50 percent, then click OK in the Mask Options dialog box.

The mask turns to green, making it easier to see the areas that are masked. The opacity of a mask lets you vary its density to make editing easier. This opacity doesn't effect *how much* something is masked (in other words, a mask set to 25 percent opacity and a mask set to 75 percent opacity both totally protect whatever is masked).

You can change the Quick Mask mode (by clicking the Selected Areas option) so that the color indicates selected, not masked, areas. For more information about the Quick Mask mode, see the *Adobe Photoshop User Guide.*

Editing the mask

Look around the edges of the pepper and you'll notice that some of the darker areas are not masked. Since you want the entire pepper to be part of the mask, you're going to use the *eraser tool* and the paintbrush tool to edit this mask.

To edit the mask:

1 Click the eraser tool in the toolbox and move the pointer into the image area. Notice that the pointer turns into an eraser.

2 Use the eraser to remove the green areas in the background.

Erasing parts of the mask removes their protection and makes them part of the selection.

3 Zoom in on the left side of the pepper.

4 Click the paintbrush tool, uncollapse the Brushes palette, and select the second brush from the left in the top row.

5 Using this fine brush, paint the edges of the pepper green.

Use short strokes, so you can easily undo part of the painting if necessary. The areas you paint turn green, adding them to the mask. Don't worry about outlining the exact shape of the pepper. What you should aim for is a soft outline of the pepper shape.

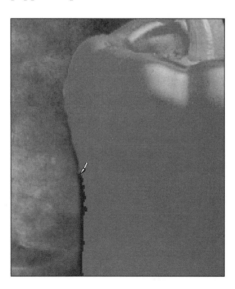

6 Move around in the image and continue to paint until all the red edges of the pepper have been added to the mask.

7 Zoom out, then click the Standard mode control in the toolbox to leave Quick Mask mode.

8 Choose Inverse from the Select menu to make the pepper the selected area.

WORKING WITH CHANNELS

Quick Mask mode temporarily creates a mask, but unless you save the mask as a selection, the mask disappears when you make another selection. You need to save this mask in a channel because you will need to use it again when you duplicate the pepper a second time.

The channels that Adobe Photoshop assigns to images are analogous to the plates used in the printing process. For example, images created using the default RGB mode have three channels— one for the red color, one for the green color, and one for the blue color.

As mentioned in Lessons 1 and 2, saved selections are also stored in channels. The channels you create to store selections are sometimes called *alpha channels*. A file can have up to 16 channels.

To display the channels in an image:

1 Choose Show Channels from the Window menu. The Channels palette appears.

TIP: YOU CAN DISPLAY INDIVIDUAL CHANNELS BY USING THE CONTROL-KEY SHORTCUTS INSTEAD OF SELECTING THE NAME IN THE CHAN-NELS PALETTE.

2 Drag the palette so that you can see the entire image.

You are currently looking at the composite channel (RGB) that shows all the color information for the image. The eye icons indicate that you are viewing the channel. The pencil icons mean that any editing you do affects that channel. You can make each individual channel visible or editable by clicking the icons.

3 Click the eye icon for the red channel.

The image changes so that now you're looking only at the blue and green information, although any editing changes would still affect the red channel. Viewing and editing individual channels lets you make very specific and subtle adjustments to an image. You'll learn more about using individual channels in Lesson 7.

4 Click the visible column for the red channel to return to the composite view of the image.

Anytime the red, blue, and green channels are all visible, you are automatically looking at the composite view of the image.

ADDING NEW CHANNELS

Although you probably don't realize it, you already know how to create new channels. Anytime you save a selection, Adobe Photoshop automatically creates a new channel (remember channel #4 and the New channel in the Save Selection submenu?). Now you're going to learn how to save and name the channels you create. The alpha channels you create are 8-bit grayscale channels within the document.

To create a channel:

1 Choose Save Selection from the Select menu.

Notice that a channel, assigned the number 4, appears in the Channels palette (any channels you create are automatically numbered sequentially).

2 Click #4 in the Channels palette to view the new channel.

Clicking a channel name makes it the only visible and editable channel. The #4 grayscale channel appears, showing you the mask you created. If you've worked with traditional masks, this image probably looks familiar. The white areas are transparent and are affected by any changes you make. The black areas are opaque and are protected from change.

3 Choose Channel Options from the Channels palette pop-up menu.

As in the Quick Mask mode, you can reverse these black-and-white settings by clicking the Selected Areas option in the Channel Options dialog box. Leave the setting at Masked Areas for now.

You can also use the painting and editing tools to edit a mask in its channel. In most cases, however, it's easier to edit the mask when you can also see the underlying image.

4 Name the channel *Pepper* and click OK.

The name appears in the Channels palette.

5 Click RGB in the Channels palette (or press Control+zero) to return to the composite view.

6 Save this file as RPEPPER1.PSD.

7 Copy the selection to the Clipboard and close the file.

Although it's a good idea to save complex selections in additional channels, channels do increase the size of your file. If you don't have much disk space, you might want to delete channels or save them to another file before saving your document. See the *Adobe Photoshop User Guide* for more information on deleting, saving, and duplicating channels.

MAKING A PATH INTO A SELECTION

Now you're ready to paste the pepper selection into your SIGN3.PSD file. In your final image, you want the pepper to be pasted *behind* the border. Normal pasting would put the pepper in front of everything else in the image. In order to paste behind, you must have an active selection in the image (so there is something to go behind). The *Border* path must be turned into a selection before you can paste behind it.

To define the path as a selection:

1 Click *Border* in the Paths palette to select this path. A check mark appears before the name.

2 Choose Make Selection from the Paths palette pop-up menu. The Make Selection dialog box appears.

3 Be sure that Feather Radius is set to 0, the Anti-aliased option is on, and New Selection is chosen, then click OK to define the path as a selection.

4 Save the selection in a new channel.

5 Double-click #4 in the Channels palette to display the Channel Options dialog box (or choose Channel Options from the Paths palette pop-up menu) and name the channel *Border*.

The channel appears in the window. This black-and-white image clearly shows you the masked areas. You will need to load this selection when you paste the second pepper into the image.

6 Click RGB in the Channels palette to return to the composite view.

7 Save the file as SIGN4.PSD to include this selection as part of the file.

PASTING ONE SELECTION BEHIND ANOTHER

With an active selection in the image, you're ready to paste the pepper from the Clipboard.

To paste the pepper:

1 Choose Paste Behind from the Edit menu.

The pepper appears behind the border in the middle of the image. The selection border for the entire selection is visible so that you can see how much of the selection is behind the border.

Since the pepper is a floating selection, you can drag it around to place it just where you want it. To see how this works, click a selection tool and drag the pepper around. Watch how different parts of the pepper are hidden by the border. When you've moved it around a few times, drag the pepper back to the middle of the image.

2 Choose Hide Edges (or press Control+H) from the Select menu.

Hiding the selection marquee can give you a better idea of how the final image will look.

ROTATING A SELECTION

In addition to dragging, another way to change the position of a floating selection is to use the Rotate command. For this image, you're going to rotate the pepper slightly to the left.

To rotate a selection:

1 Choose Rotate from the Image menu and Free from the submenu.

A box appears around the selection with four corner handles.

2 Drag the top-left handle down until the pepper is tilted at a slight angle (use the angle of the left pepper in the final image as a guide).

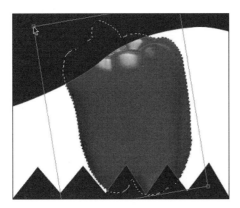

Be patient! It takes a few seconds for Adobe Photoshop to show you a preview of the new orientation. You can keep adjusting the handles until you have the angle you want. Notice that the selection border edges reappear when you choose Rotate.

3 Move the pointer around in the image and pass it over the rotation box.

When you're inside the box, you see a *gavel icon*. When you're outside the box, you see the *No icon*. Clicking when the gavel icon is visible (inside the box) confirms the rotation; clicking when the No icon is visible (outside the box) lets you change your mind and cancel the rotation.

4 Click with the gavel icon to rotate the image.

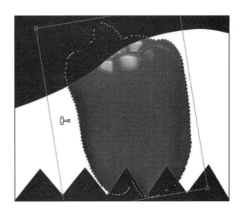

5 Click the rectangular marquee tool, then drag the pepper down until it is almost a quarter of an inch from the left edge of the window and the tip of the pepper stem is slightly below the 2-1/2-inch marker.

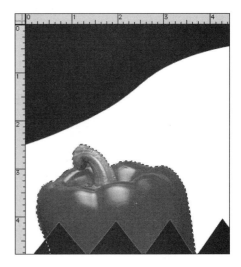

6 Save the file as SIGN5.PSD.

POSTERIZING THE IMAGE

The Posterize command lets you change the number of gray levels (or brightness values) for an image. In effect, this produces large, flat areas in an image.

To posterize the pepper:

1 Choose Map from the Image menu and Posterize from the submenu. The Posterize dialog box appears.

2 Drag the dialog box so you can see how the pepper changes.

3 Set the number of levels to 3 and click the Preview option.

4 Click OK to posterize the image.

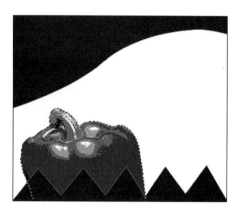

PASTING THE SECOND PEPPER

Now follow the same steps to paste the second pepper into the image, rotate it, and posterize it.

To paste the pepper:

1 In the SIGN5.PSD image, choose Load Selection to load the Border selection again (remember, you must have an active selection to paste behind).

2 Choose Paste Behind.

3 Rotate the pepper to the right, then drag so that the tip of the stem is about 4-1/4 inches from the left edge of the window and 1-1/4 inches from the top of the window (part of the pepper will extend beyond the right edge and bottom of the window).

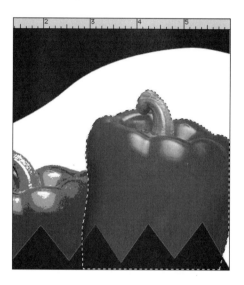

4 Choose Map from the Image menu and Posterize from the submenu. Posterize the selection using 3 Levels.

5 Deselect the pepper.

DRAWING A NON-CONTIGUOUS PATH

The path you drew for the border consisted of a set of continuous connected lines. You can also draw a path that is a series of segments. To finish the border on this image, you're going to draw a non-contiguous path.

To draw the path:

1 Click the pen tool in the Paths palette.

2 Click the gray area in the Paths palette to deselect the current path as you begin a new border.

3 Click in the lower-left corner of the image, about a quarter of an inch to the left of the first triangle.

4 Click the next point near the tip of the first triangle. This creates the first path segment.

5 Click the pen tool in the Paths palette to end that segment.

6 Click slightly to the right of the first triangle tip, then click near the bottom of the triangle.

7 Click the first point in this segment to close the segment. You will see the loop that indicates closing a path.

There are two ways to end a path segment; you can either click the first anchor point in the segment, or click the pen tool before beginning the next segment. If you don't end a segment, a line will always be drawn between the last two points you clicked.

8 Continue drawing the segments until you've outlined the bottom border.

The exact location of the segments isn't important; use your own creative judgment.

9 Choose Save Path from the Paths palette pop-up menu and name the path Lines.

10 Save the file.

STROKING A PATH

Stroking a path allows you to paint color along the path border. You can choose to apply the paint with any of the painting tools in the toolbox.

To stroke the path:

1 Click the eyedropper in the pepper stem to sample the green as the new foreground color.

2 Click the paintbrush tool and make sure the Opacity in the Brushes palette is set to 100 percent.

3 Double-click the second brush from the left in the top row of the Brushes palette to display the Brush Options dialog box. Set the Diameter to 3, the Hardness to 0, and the Spacing to 25 percent, then click OK.

4 Choose Stroke Path from the Paths palette pop-up menu.

The path is outlined in green paint.

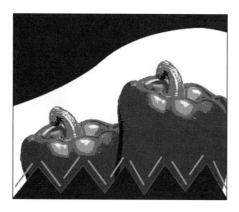

5 Click a blank area of the Paths palette scroll box to deselect the path.

Since changes to the current path are automatically saved, if you don't deselect the path you'll add to the *Lines* path the next time you begin drawing with the pen tool.

FILLING A SUBPATH WITH A PATTERN

You might remember that when you created the *Border* path it consisted of two subpaths—the top border and the bottom border. To achieve more balance in this image, you're going to change the fill in the top subpath to a pattern.

To fill a subpath:

1 Open the MEZZDOT.EPS file in the LESSON4 directory. Accept the EPS Rasterizer default values and click OK to display the file.

2 Choose All from the Select menu to select the entire image.

3 Choose Define Pattern from the Edit menu to copy the pattern to the pattern buffer, then close the file.

4 Click *Border* in the Paths palette to select the path.

5 With the arrow tool in the Paths palette selected, click the top subpath to display its anchor points.

6 Choose Fill Subpath from the Paths palette pop-up menu. (Notice that the name now reads *sub-path* since only part of a path is selected.)

7 Make sure that Pattern is selected, Opacity is set to 100 percent, and Normal Mode is chosen, then click OK.

The pattern replaces the dark blue of the former fill.

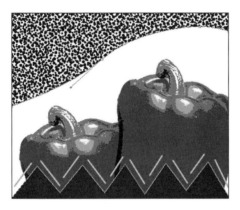

8 In the Colors palette, create a foreground color with an R value of about 199, a G value of about 199, and a B value of about 38.

9 Choose Fill Subpath again and select the Foreground Color option, set the Opacity to 100 percent, choose Lighten from the Mode menu, and click OK.

The pattern turns a khaki green. The Lighten option fills only pixels that are darker than the fill color, so the white from the original pattern remains.

10 Save this file as SIGN6.PSD.

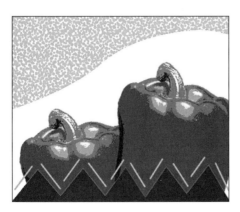

ADDING TRANSPARENT TYPE

In Lessons 2 and 3, you added opaque type to the images. In this image, you're going to make the type transparent. You'll then fill the translucent type with a gradient.

To add the type:

1 Click the type tool in the toolbox and set the Opacity on the Brushes palette to 1 percent.

This makes the type transparent. You need to have transparent type so that the background can show through the gradient fill.

2 Click the insertion point in the upper-left corner of the image.

3 Choose Times from the Font pop-up menu and enter 42 points for the type size.

4 Enter 45 for the Leading option and 13 for the Spacing option, under Style check Bold and Italic and set the Alignment to Left.

If you've used the type tool in other applications, you're probably familiar with these two options. Leading, or *line spacing*, is the measurement from baseline to baseline. Spacing, or *kerning*, controls the spacing between letters.

5 Type **pimientos** in the first line of the text box, press Return, insert three blank spaces, and type **rescos** in the second line. Both words should be in lowercase.

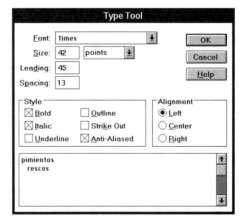

When you want type to extend over more than one line, you must press Return to indicate where you want the type to break. The blank characters in the second line are there to space the type correctly, and leave room for the *f*, which will be in a different style and type size.

6 Click OK to close the dialog box.

7 Move the arrow pointer over the *p* in *pimientos* and drag until the bottom-left edge of the letter is three-quarters of an inch from the top of the window and half an inch from the left edge.

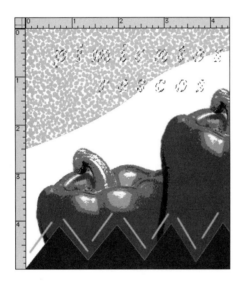

FILLING TYPE WITH A GRADIENT

To fill the type, you must first choose the foreground and background colors for the gradient.

To fill the type:

1 Use the eyedropper to sample the bright red surrounding the highlights in a pepper for the foreground color.

2 Hold down the Alt key and sample the blue in the bottom border for the background color.

3 Choose Defloat from the Select menu to defloat the type (or press Control+J).

If you try to fill the selected type while it is still floating, you won't see any change because the type is only 1-percent opaque. (Choose Float from the Select menu and use the gradient fill tool if you want to check this out. Be sure to defloat the type before proceeding.)

When you defloat the type, you allow the gradient fill to mix with the underlying pixels in the image, blending the pixels together and producing the see-through effect.

4 Click the gradient tool.

5 Drag the Opacity setting on the Brushes palette to 90 percent.

6 Drag diagonally from the top of the *m* in *pimientos* to the bottom of the *c* in *rescos*.

The type is filled with the gradient.

COMBINING FONTS IN TYPE

Often, you want the type in a design to be uniform and easy to read, so that the type does not distract from the graphic impact of the image. Sometimes, however, you can use the type as a design element itself, by combining type of different fonts, styles, and sizes. In this display sign, the type is more graphic than informational. You're going to complete the sign by adding the flowing *f* in the second line of type.

To add the remaining character:

1 Click the type tool, then click the insertion point to the left of the *r* in *rescos.* The Type Tool dialog box appears.

2 Set the Font to Times Italic, the Size to 90 points, and enter 0 for the Leading and Spacing.

3 Type a lowercase **f** in the text box, and click OK.

4 Drag the *f* until its top edge is under the left edge of the *m* in *pimientos.*

Use the placement in the reference file as a guide. None of the letter should extend below the top border.

5 Drag the Opacity slider in the Brushes palette and watch the letter become more opaque. Stop when you like the effect.

6 Deselect the text.

7 Save this image as SIGN7.PSD.

8 Make sure that you are correctly routed to the printer you plan to print to. Choose Print from the File menu if you want to print a copy of the image.

9 Close the files.

You've come a long way! In just four lessons you've learned how to create a very professional-looking piece of art. Along the way, you've built up quite a working knowledge of paths, masks, and channels.

LE MONDE

B

Gourmet Visions

Lesson

5

LESSON 5: MANIPULATING SELECTIONS

This lesson marks your leap from beginning to experienced Adobe Photoshop user. In this lesson, you'll make selections from five different files and paste them into a new file to create a composite image. As part of building this image, you'll refine your pasting and selecting skills and learn more about using the pen tool, stroking, and filling. It should take you about two hours to complete this lesson.

Source file (ASPARAGU.PSD)

In this lesson, you'll learn how to do the following:

- scale a selection

- change the hue and saturation of a selection

- apply filters to selections

- stroke a selection

- make selections using the pen tool

- paste using the composite controls

- defringe a selection

- adjust a selection's brightness and contrast

- flip a selection

- paint with a pattern

- edit type in a channel

At the end of this lesson you'll have created the cover for an informative food brochure that Gourmet Visions is distributing as a public service to its customers. The source graphics for this cover art include both line art and full-color continuous-tone images.

Source file (PLATE.PSD)

Source file (VEGGIES.PSD)

Source file (FISH.PSD)

Ending image (BROCHURE.PSD)

BEGINNING THIS LESSON

As in the last lesson, you will open a new file and the final image for this lesson.

To begin this lesson:

1 Open the BROCHURE.PSD file in the LESSON5 directory and turn on the rulers in this window.

2 Zoom out to reduce the image, resize the window, then drag the window to the upper-right corner of your screen.

3 Collapse the Brushes, Paths, Color, and Channel palettes to give yourself more working room. You might want to line up the palettes along the bottom of your screen.

4 Choose New from the File menu and create an RGB Color file that's 4.6 inches wide and 4.6 inches high with a resolution of 72.

5 Turn on the rulers in the untitled window and save this file in your Projects directory as COVER1.PSD.

CREATING THE BACKGROUND

Your first step is to design a graphic background for the bottom half of the cover. The background begins with a straightforward selection from a photograph of asparagus and ends with an interesting textured pattern.

To copy and paste the selection:

1 Open the ASPARAGU.PSD file in the LESSON5 directory and turn on the rulers in this window.

2 Click the rectangular marquee tool and hold down the Shift key as you select about a three-quarter-inch square section of the asparagus from the upper third of the bunch.

The exact location of the selection doesn't matter; in fact, the final effect will be unique to the selection you make. Just be sure the selection includes some light and dark areas. If you need to change the selected area, hold down the Control and Alt keys and drag the selection border.

3 Copy the selection to the Clipboard, then deselect the selection.

Leave this file open for now, as you'll use another selection from it later in the lesson.

4 Click the COVER1.PSD window to make it active (or choose COVER1.PSD from the Window menu).

5 Paste the selection.

Since there is no active selection, the pasted selection appears in the middle of the file.

6 Drag the selection until it's near the upper-right corner of the window.

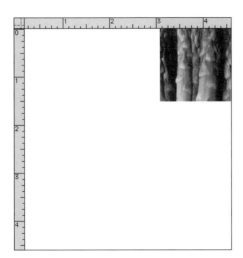

7 Choose Hide Edges from the Select menu to hide the selection borders so you can place the selection more precisely.

8 Use the up arrow and right arrow keys to move the selection until it's flush with the top and right edges of the window.

Each press of an arrow key moves the selection one pixel at a time. This lets you get to the exact edge of the window without inadvertently losing part of the selection outside the top or right side of the window.

SCALING THE SELECTION

Scaling lets you extend or shrink the length and width of a selection. Depending on the effect you're trying to achieve, you can keep the original proportions, or you can distort the selection as you scale.

You're going to scale the selection so that it fills the entire window. Don't worry about the fact that this area is only a small part of the final image—you'll learn how to add the extra space later in this lesson.

To scale the selection:

1 Choose Effects from the Image menu and Scale from the submenu.

A box appears around the selection with four corner handles (you might remember these handles from the Rotate command).

2 Drag the bottom-left handle down and to the left until the selection fills the window. A preview of the scaled selection appears.

3 Click with the gavel icon to confirm the scaling.

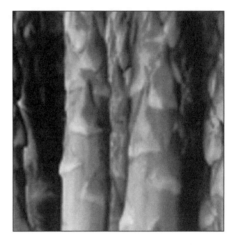

4 Deselect the selection.

5 Save the file as COVER2.PSD.

ADJUSTING THE HUE AND SATURATION

Right now, the selection just looks like some stretched-out stalks of asparagus. For the food brochure, you'd like the background texture to be a bit more abstract. To achieve this touch of unreality, you're going to change the hue, saturation, and lightness of the selection.

Hue is the name of the color that places it in the correct location in the color spectrum. For example, a color with a blue hue is distinguished from a yellow, red, or green color.

Saturation refers to the clarity or degree of hue in a color. A neutral white, gray, or black doesn't have any saturation, so saturation is also a measure of how much a color differs from neutral gray. Less saturation produces a color closer to neutral; more saturation produces a color farther from neutral. Saturation is usually described using such words as *faint, pale, vivid,* or *strong.* For example, a selection might be dull red, bright red, or brilliant red depending on its saturation.

Lightness, or *brightness,* describes the intensity of light as it is reflected from, or transmitted by, the color. For example, hair color might be described as light brown, medium brown, or dark brown.

To change the hue, saturation, and lightness:

1 Choose Adjust from the Image menu and Hue/Saturation from the submenu (or press Control+U). The Hue/Saturation dialog box appears.

2 Drag the dialog box down to the bottom of the screen and, if necessary, select the Preview check box so you can watch the changes as you move the sliders.

3 Drag the Hue slider to the right until it reads 63.

The asparagus takes on more of a neon green hue.

4 Drag the Hue slider all the way to the left until it reads –180.

Now the asparagus is a rather interesting (if unappetizing) purple hue. The hue values (in this case, +63 and –180) reflect the number of degrees of rotation around the color wheel that the new color is from the pixel's original color. A positive value indicates clockwise rotation; a negative value indicates counterclockwise rotation.

If you've used the Apple Color Picker, you're already familiar with the idea of the color wheel. For more information about the color wheel and the hue setting, see the *Adobe Photoshop User Guide.*

5 Return the Hue slider to 0.

6 Drag the Saturation slider to the right until it reads +56.

The asparagus increases in saturation and takes on an unreal glow as the colors become very intense.

7 Drag the Saturation slider to the left until it reads –56.

The asparagus decreases in saturation and is now an almost gray, dull green. Dragging the Saturation slider to the right shifts the color *away* from the center of the color wheel. Dragging the slider to the left shifts the color *toward* the center of the color wheel. If you want to, take a few minutes to experiment with changing the hue and saturation in this Preview mode. It doesn't matter what values you end up with.

As this practice has shown you, you can invent a wide variety of colors by adjusting hue and saturation from the starting point of the selection's original color. Sometimes, however, when you want to dramatically change the color of a selection, it's easier to start from zero than to modify an existing color.

Colorizing the selection

The Colorize option lets you use the Hue and Saturation sliders to change a selection's color based on rotation from the 0-degree point on the color wheel (which is red). When you're using the Colorize option, positive numbers indicate counterclockwise motion and negative numbers indicate clockwise motion around the wheel.

TIP: FOR A BRIEF
DESCRIPTION OF
EACH INSTALLED FIL-
TER, CHOOSE ABOUT
PLUG-IN FROM THE
HELP MENU; THEN
CHOOSE THE FILTER
FROM THE SUBMENU.
CLICK TO CLOSE THE
DESCRIPTION BOX.

To use the Colorize option:

1 Select the Colorize option.

The window turns red to indicate that the value you're specifying is a specific number of degrees from red in the color wheel. The Hue is set to 0 and the Saturation is set to 100.

2 Type +41 into the Hue text box and leave the Saturation at 100 percent.

The asparagus takes on a gold color, since gold is approximately 41 degrees from red (in a counter-clockwise direction) on the color wheel.

3 Set the Lightness to –27.

Changing the lightness setting provides a more muted golden color. Now this selection is close to the color needed for the final image.

4 Click OK to change the hue and lightness.

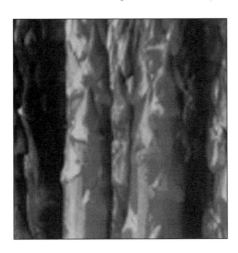

5 Save the file.

FILTERING THE SELECTION

Filters provide one of the easiest and quickest ways to create visually exciting results. Adobe Photoshop comes with a wide variety of filters that let you produce some stunning special effects. Plug-in filters for Adobe Photoshop are also available from third-party companies.

As the final step in creating your background texture, you're going to use a filter to add *noise* (pixels with randomly distributed color values) to the image.

To apply a filter:

1 Choose Noise from the Filter menu and Add Noise from the submenu. The Add Noise dialog box appears.

2 Set the Amount to 32, click the Gaussian option, then click OK to apply the filter.

The Gaussian option distributes color values of noise along a bell-shaped curve. This multicolored effect is just what you want for the final background texture; however, you want to tone down the effect slightly.

3 Choose Stylize from the Filter menu and Diffuse from the submenu. The Diffuse dialog box appears.

4 Click Lighten Only, then click OK.

The Diffuse filter shuffles pixels to make a selection look less focused. The Lighten Only option replaces dark pixels with lighter pixels. As you can see, applying multiple filters allows you to create an even wider assortment of unique effects.

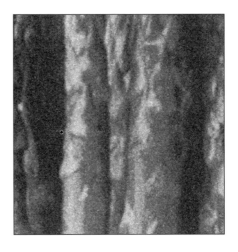

5 Save the file.

STROKING A SELECTION

In the last lesson, you learned to stroke a path, which outlined the path with color. You can also stroke a selection to add a strip of color around the edge of the selection. You could achieve this same effect by using the Border command, then filling the border you create, but stroking is faster.

Before you add the border, you're going to add a plate to the selection, then you'll stroke the entire selection.

To copy the plate:

1 Open the PLATE.PSD file in the LESSON5 directory.

2 Double-click the magic wand tool and set the tolerance to 64, then click the magic wand anywhere in the gray area outside the plate.

Because of the distinct color differences, this produces an almost perfect selection of the entire background.

3 If you need to add to the selection, use the lasso with the Shift key to add any missing sections of the background to the selection. The silverware should not be included in the selection.

4 Inverse the selection so that the plate is selected.

Use your function key for this command if you assigned one in the last lesson.

5 Copy the selection, close the file, and paste the plate into the COVER2.PSD image.

Notice that as you paste, the plate becomes the active selection, replacing the selection border

that was around the entire image. Remember, when you create or paste a new selection, it replaces any existing selection.

The plate is very large in relation to the rest of the image. This is because the resolution of the PLATE.PSD file is 144, while the resolution of the COVER2.PSD file is 72. You'll learn more about resolution and resizing when you're cutting and pasting in Lesson 10.

6 Drag the selection down and to the right until you can't see the knife and fork (the top of the plate and the left edge of the plate should both be at about the 1-inch marker on the rulers).

7 Choose All from the Select menu to select the entire image.

Now you're ready to add the border.

To stroke the selection:

1 Click the default colors icon to set the foreground color to black.

2 Choose Stroke from the Edit menu. The Stroke dialog box appears.

3 Enter 4 for the Width under Stroke and click the Inside option under Location. Leave the Opacity at 100 percent and the Mode at Normal under Blending.

4 Click OK to stroke the selection.

A black border appears around the image. Since the selection fills the entire image, you want to start stroking from the inside edge of the selection and move in for a width of 4 pixels. See the *Adobe Photoshop User Guide* for an explanation of the other stroke options.

5 Save the file.

KEEPING TRACK OF FILE SIZE

As a final step in creating this part of the cover, you're going to add space around the image, so you will have room to add the vegetables that overlap the outside of the textured background. This increase in canvas size is an interim step toward the final size of the image (which will be the actual size of the brochure). As you're working with an Adobe Photoshop file, it's always a good idea to keep the file size as small as possible. Using a file that's bigger than you need slows down your procedures, especially when you're applying special effects like scaling and filters.

To add the canvas around the image:

1 Choose Canvas Size from the Image menu and enter 5.6 inches for the Width and 5.6 inches for the Height of the new canvas.

Look at the file size at the top of the Current Size and New Size boxes. Adding just an inch all the way around the image increases the file size from 321K to 476K.

2 Make sure the center placement box is selected, then click OK.

The new canvas is added to the edges of the image. As the finishing touch, you're going to create a slightly *underwater* look to this image.

3 Choose Distort from the Filter menu and Ripple from the submenu. The Ripple dialog box appears.

4 Enter 30 for the Amount and select the Large option to increase the ripple frequency, then click OK.

That's the look you want! The ripple is especially noticeable around the border.

5 Save the file as COVER3.PSD.

TIP: YOU CAN ALSO
HOLD DOWN THE CON-
TROL KEY WHILE THE
PEN TOOL IS SELECTED
TO DISPLAY THE
ARROW POINTER.

MAKING SELECTIONS WITH THE PEN TOOL

In the last lesson, you used the pen tool to draw freehand paths. You can also use the pen tool to draw irregularly shaped paths composed of curves and straight lines. These paths can then be saved as selections. The next element to be added to the brochure cover is an asparagus stalk, which you'll select using the pen tool.

To select using the pen tool:

1 Choose ASPARAGU.PSD from the Window menu (or click the window to make it active). If you've closed the ASPARAGU.PSD file, reopen it.

2 Choose Zoom In from the Window menu.

You're going to select the center stalk in the asparagus bunch. When you're making a complex selection like this, it's sometimes preferable to start with an approximation of the shape and then zoom in to edit the individual anchor points.

3 Uncollapse the Paths palette and click the pen tool.

4 Starting at the very tip of the center stalk, click once to set the first anchor point.

5 Move down along the right edge of the stalk and drag to add a curved segment at the corner of the asparagus tip.

6 Move down about half an inch along the right edge of the stalk, and click to add a straight segment.

7 Move down about 2 inches and click to add another straight segment.

It's okay if this straight-line path segment cuts off part of the stalk. You'll come back and adjust this point later.

8 Continue adding straight segments until you have moved down the right side of the stalk, across the bottom of the stalk, and up the left edge. Stop when you are about equal with the curved segment on the right side (the second anchor point you clicked).

9 Drag to add a curved segment at this point across from the other curved segment.

10 Close the path by clicking the first anchor point.

Editing the path

Since it takes a little practice to get used to the pen tool, you might not be totally happy with the selection border you've drawn.

Editing straight segments of the path is simple. You just click the arrow tool in the Paths palette and drag to adjust the anchor points.

The anchor points you use when drawing a curve are *smooth* anchor points (both points at the end of the direction line move in unison when you drag). When you want to modify the two halves of a direction line independently, you change the anchor point to a *corner* point (the direction points move independently). To understand how this works, try editing a segment of the path at the top of the asparagus stalk.

To edit a curved segment:

1 Zoom in on the asparagus stalk so you can see the path clearly.

2 Select the arrow tool and click the anchor point for the curved segment (the second point you placed). The direction lines appear.

3 Drag either direction point.

Notice that the handles move in unison around the anchor point.

4 Click the corner tool in the Paths palette (the tool on the far right) and click the anchor point.

This turns the point into a corner point with no direction lines.

5 Click the anchor point and drag to make the direction lines appear again.

6 Drag the top direction point.

Notice that the direction points now move independently, and you're adjusting either the segment on the path from the first anchor point or the segment leading from this anchor point. Once you release the direction point, the anchor point reverts to a smooth point (the direction points move in unison). Clicking the corner tool on an anchor point toggles the anchor point between a smooth point and a corner point.

7 Toggling between a corner point and a smooth point, drag the direction points until the curve is the way you want it.

8 Experiment with using the corner tool to toggle the anchor point of the curved segment on the left side of the stalk as you make adjustments to this curve.

You can also use the corner tool to make corrections to straight-line segments.

To edit a straight segment:

1 Select the corner tool from the Paths palette and click the third point you placed (the one that is below the curved segment).

This turns the smooth point into a corner point so you can use direction lines to adjust the path.

2 Drag to make the direction lines appear, and adjust the point.

3 Toggle the anchor points a few times to see how the direction points switch between moving together and moving independently.

Adding and deleting points in a path

The pen tools with the plus and minus signs in the Paths palette allow you to add and delete points on a path.

To add and delete anchor points:

1 Click the pen+ tool in the Paths palette and move the pointer onto the path between two of the long straight segments along the stalk.

When you are directly over the path, a plus sign appears next to the pen pointer.

2 Click the path.

An anchor point with a direction line appears.

3 Add a few more anchor points to the path.

4 Click the pen tool in the Paths palette and move the pointer over one of the points you just added.

When you're directly over an anchor point, a minus sign appears next to the pen pointer.

5 Click to delete the point from the path.

If you want to experiment with these tools, add and delete points until the path is the way you want it.

6 Choose Make Selection from the Paths palette pop-up menu, set the Feather Radius to 0, make sure the Anti-aliased option is on, choose New Selection, and click OK.

7 Click a selection tool, then click anywhere outside the path to deselect the path (the marquee will still be around the selection).

8 Uncollapse the Channel palette, then save the selection in channel #4 and name it *Asparagus*.

You will be copying this selection several times, and in case there's a problem with the copying, you wouldn't want to have to select this complex shape again.

9 Return to the composite view and save this file as A1.PSD (saving now ensures that the selection is saved as part of the file).

10 Copy the asparagus selection to the Clipboard and close the file. It's OK to close the file without saving the path since you've saved the *Asparagus* selection.

USING COMPOSITE CONTROLS

Normally, when you paste a selection, every pixel in the floating selection is visible after the pasting process. Using the Composite Controls command, you can indicate which pixels in the floating selection will replace the pixels in the underlying image. This allows you to "composite" (or blend) the selection into the image.

You can also change the opacity of the pasted selection. Take a look at the final image. Using the composite controls, you are now going to create the "fade-away" look of the three asparagus stalks.

To paste the first two stalks:

1 Activate the COVER3.PSD window and paste the selection.

The selection appears in the center of the window.

2 Choose Rotate from the Image menu and 90 degrees CW from the submenu.

3 Drag the selection up and to the left until its width is centered around the 1-inch marker and the tip of the stalk is at the 3-inch marker.

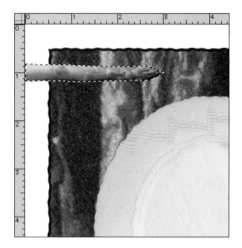

4 Save the file.

This first paste of the stalk selection is a normal paste—that is, all the pixels in the pasted selection are visible and the selection is totally opaque.

5 Copy the selection to the Clipboard to retain the new orientation of the selection.

6 Choose Paste from the Edit menu to paste the second stalk.

A second stalk appears over the first selection. When you paste into a window with no active selection, the pasted selection appears in the center of the window. When you paste into a window and there is an active selection, the pasted selection appears *over* the current selection. In this case, you can see this clearly, since the pasted selection is in a different location from the already pasted stalk (you've dragged some of the original selection outside the window). When the pasted and current selections are identical, you can't see any change in the window when you paste.

7 Drag the selection down until the top of the second stalk is about half an inch below the bottom of the first stalk, then line up the tips of the stalks.

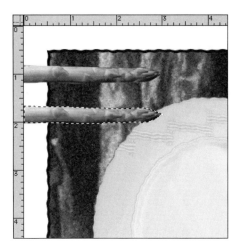

Determining which pixels are visible

Currently, all of the pasted pixels are visible for both pasted selections. Now, you're going to experiment with the second stalk to see how composite controls work.

To paste using composite controls:

1 Choose Composite Controls from the Edit menu. The Composite Controls dialog box appears.

2 Make sure the Preview option is selected, and drag the dialog box to the bottom of the screen so you can see the changes as you move the sliders.

3 Drag the black triangle under the Floating slider to the right, until it reads 85.

The values of the pixels in a selection can range from 0 (black) to 255 (white). The Floating slider controls which pixels in the floating selection replace the underlying pixels.

As you drag the triangle, the selection begins to break up and part of it is no longer visible. Dragging the black triangle tells Adobe Photoshop not to display the pixels in the floating selection that have a value between 0 and 85 (these are the dark pixels).

4 Return the black triangle to 0 and drag the white triangle under the Floating slider to the left, until it reads 165.

Notice that now the lighter pixels (those with a value between 165 and 255) are not visible.

5 Return the white triangle to 255.

6 Drag the black triangle under the Underlying slider to the right, until it reads 64.

The Underlying slider determines which pixels in the underlying image replace the pixels in the floating selection. In this case, all the pixels in the underlying area that have a value between 0 and 65 replace the pixels in the floating selection. You can see this clearly if you look at the border where it intersects the asparagus stalk. The border in the underlying image cuts right through the second stalk.

7 Return the black triangle to 0 and experiment with the white triangle under the Underlying slider, to see how the lighter pixels in the underlying image replace the pixels in the floating selection.

Look at the border area again to see how the white canvas area replaces the bottom half of a stalk as soon as you begin to move the white triangle to the right.

8 When you've finished exploring, return the white triangle to 255.

CHANGING THE OPACITY OF A PASTED SELECTION

To be able to *see through* the asparagus stalks, you want all the pixels to be visible, but you want to create a dimming effect. To do this, you change the opacity of the floating selection.

To change the opacity:

1 Enter a value of 70 in the Opacity text box in the Composite Controls dialog box, then click OK.

This changes the selection so that it is dimmed, but all the pixels are visible. Look again at the area where the white canvas is under the selection. You can see how this creates a different effect from replacing the pixels with those in the underlying area.

2 Paste the selection again and drag the third stalk down about half an inch under the second stalk and line up the tips.

3 Choose Composite Controls again and set the Opacity for the third stalk to 45 percent, then click OK to close the dialog box.

4 Save the file as COVER4.PSD.

USING THE FEATHER COMMAND

As you learned in Lesson 2, feathering blurs the edges of a selection by building a transition boundary between the selection and the surrounding pixels. You can feather the edges as you make a selection by using the Feather Radius option in the Rectangular Marquee Options and Elliptical Marquee Options dialog boxes, as you did in Lesson 2.

You can also feather a selection after it is made, but before you copy and paste it. Feathering is apparent only when you modify a selection by cutting, moving, pasting, or filling it.

Anti-aliasing is another technique that softens the edges of a selection. See the *Adobe Photoshop User Guide* for a discussion and comparison of feathering and anti-aliasing.

To feather a selection:

1 Open the VEGGIES.PSD file in the LESSON5 directory.

In this file, both the radish and the tomato have been saved as selections.

2 Choose Load Selection from the Select menu and Radish from the submenu.

3 Zoom in twice on the radish so you can see the feathering effect more clearly. The feathering will be particularly clear on the radish tail.

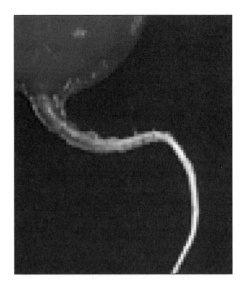

4 Choose Feather from the Select menu. The Feather dialog box appears.

5 Enter 3 for the Feather Radius.

This is too much feathering. You can see that the white section of the tail is no longer in the selection.

6 Choose Undo Feather, then choose Feather again and enter 1 for the Feather Radius.

Watch carefully as the colors blend to smooth out the selection border.

7 Zoom out to return the VEGGIES.PSD file to a 1:1 view.

8 Copy the radish to the Clipboard, then paste the radish into the COVER4.PSD window.

The pasted radish is dramatically out of proportion to the asparagus stalks. To make the relative sizes of the vegetables more realistic, you need to scale the radish selection.

MEASURING SCALING PERCENTAGES WITH THE INFO PALETTE

The Info palette provides information about the location of the pointer in the window and the color values of the pixel at the current pointer location. You'll learn more about using this palette to measure color in Lesson 7.

Depending on the tool you're using, the Info palette provides more than just the *X* and *Y* coordinates of the pointer. It can also tell you dimensions, distance, angle of rotation, and percentage of scaling. You're going to use this scale information as you scale the radish selection.

To display the Info palette:

1 Choose Show Info from the Window menu. The Info palette appears. (If you have function keys, you can press F8 to display this palette.)

2 Drag the Info palette off the COVER4.PSD window.

3 Move the pointer around in the window and watch the *X* and *Y* values change.

The pointer location is given in the current ruler units. The width and height measurements are the size of the floating selection.

4 Choose Effects from the Image menu and Scale from the submenu.

The selection is surrounded by the effects box with four corner handles. Notice that two angle measurements appear at the bottom of the Info palette.

5 Hold down the Shift key to constrain the scaling, and drag the lower-left handle up until the Info palette reads about 55 percent.

6 Click inside the selection with the gavel icon to confirm the scaling.

7 Click a selection tool and then drag the selection to the upper-right corner of the background, so that the edges of the leaves slightly overlap the top border of the textured area. (Use the final image as a placement reference.)

ADJUSTING BRIGHTNESS AND CONTRAST

As the final step in adding the radish to the brochure cover, you're going to adjust the brightness and contrast of the selection.

Brightness, as mentioned earlier in this lesson, describes the intensity of light reflected from or transmitted through an image. *Contrast* is a measure of the tonal gradation between the highlights, midtones, and shadows in the selection or image.

To adjust the brightness and contrast:

1 Choose Adjust from the Image menu and Brightness/Contrast from the submenu (or press Control+B). The Brightness/Contrast dialog box appears.

2 Make sure the Preview option is selected, then drag the dialog box down, so you can see the changes as you move the sliders.

3 Experiment with brightness by dragging the slider to the left to decrease the brightness, and to the right to increase the brightness.

You can see that the radish gets dull, or more vivid, depending on the direction in which you drag.

4 Type in +24 for the Brightness.

5 Experiment with the contrast by dragging its slider to the left to decrease the contrast, and to the right to increase the contrast.

Decreasing the contrast makes the green of the leaves closer to the red of the radish itself (they both become more neutral colors). Increasing the contrast makes these two areas stand out more sharply.

6 Set the Contrast to +24 also.

7 Click OK to put the settings into effect.

8 Deselect the radish, then save the file as COVER5.PSD.

DEFRINGING A SELECTION

When you paste a smooth-edged selection, some of the pixels surrounding the selection border are included with the selection. *Defringing* a selection replaces the color of any fringe pixels with the colors of nearby pixels in the selection that contain pure colors (pure colors don't contain any of the background color). You are going to defringe the tomatoes as you complete your assembly of vegetables for the brochure cover.

To defringe a selection:

1 Return to the VEGGIES.PSD image and load the Tomato selection.

2 Copy the selection to the Clipboard and close the VEGGIES.PSD file.

You defringe a selection after it is pasted.

3 Paste the tomato into the COVER5.PSD image.

4 Zoom in twice on the tomato and hide the selection borders so you can see the changes as you defringe.

Look closely at the edges of the tomato (especially the green stem borders at the top). You can see that some of the black background from the VEG-GIES.PSD file has been copied.

5 Choose Defringe from the Select menu. The Defringe dialog box appears. Move the box if necessary so you can see the tomato.

6 Enter 2 for the Width and click OK.

If the change was too subtle for you to see, choose Undo Defringe and Redo Defringe to look at the results again. The black around the edges of the selection is removed.

7 Choose Show Edges to display the selection border, then zoom out to the 1:1 view.

8 Click a selection tool and drag the tomato until it is just about a quarter of an inch under the bottom stalk of asparagus and overlaps the edge of the plate.

FLIPPING A SELECTION

You need to add one more tomato to the image. In addition to pasting and defringing this selection, you're going to add a little visual interest by flipping the second selection.

To flip a selection:

1 Choose Paste again to place a second copy of the tomato over the first selection.

2 Choose Defringe from the Select menu and enter a Width of 2.

3 Choose Flip from the Image menu and Horizontal from the submenu.

The Horizontal option flips the selection along the vertical axis. You can see that the stem in the top selection is now pointing in the opposite direction and the tomato is angled to the left.

4 Drag the tomato down so that it is under the first tomato, leaving about three-eighths of an inch between the bottom of the first tomato and the red top of the second tomato.

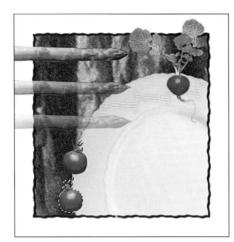

5 Click anywhere outside the selection to deselect it, then save the file.

ADDING COLOR TO A BLACK-AND-WHITE IMAGE

The final healthy food group you're going to add to the brochure cover is protein—that is, the fish. The original fish image is a line-art drawing that you'll add color to before copying it into the brochure cover.

To fill using a mode:

1 Open the FISH.PSD file in the LESSON5 directory.

2 Click the magic wand tool in the white area to select the background.

3 Choose Inverse from the Select menu.

4 Uncollapse the Colors palette to change the foreground color. Set the R slider to 54, the G slider to 0, and the B slider to 61 to produce a dark violet color.

5 Choose Fill from the Edit menu. The Fill dialog box appears. Make sure the Foreground Color option is selected, the Opacity is set to 100 percent, and the Lighten mode is selected, then click OK.

The Lighten mode fills only pixels that are darker than the foreground color. The lighter pixels do not change.

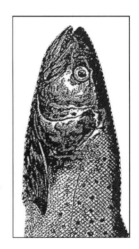

6 Save this file to the Projects directory as FISH1.PSD.

7 Copy the selection to the Clipboard, then close the file.

8 Paste the fish into the COVER5.PSD file.

9 Position the pointer on the fish's mouth and drag down until the top of the head is 2-3/4 inches from the top of the window and the mouth is about 3-3/4 inches from the left edge of the window.

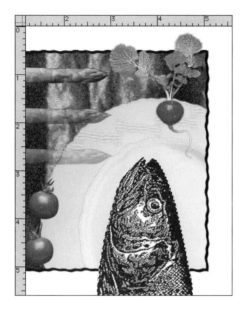

CHANGING THE IMAGE SIZE

With this selection completed, you have finished adding art to the brochure cover. Now you only need to add the top border and the type.

You have been working with the art as a 5.6-inch square image. In order to complete this project, you must resize the image so that it reflects the size of the art in the final brochure cover.

To resize the image:

1 If necessary, set the background color to white. The canvas you'll add appears in the background color.

2 Choose Image Size from the Image menu. The Image Size dialog box appears.

3 Make sure the Constrain Proportion option is checked and the Constrain File Size option is turned off.

If you constrain the file size when you resize an image, Adobe Photoshop makes sure that no pixel information is lost. This means that if you make an image smaller, the resolution is increased. If you make the image larger, the resolution is decreased. You'll learn more about the relationship between image size and resolution in Lesson 8. The *Adobe Photoshop User Guide* also provides detailed information on image size and resolution.

Sometimes, especially when printing a color image, it's important that you keep all the pixel information, and you will want the File Size option to be on. In this case, it's okay to lose some information when you make the image smaller.

4 Enter 3.2 in the Width box.

Since the Proportions option is on, Adobe Photoshop automatically enters 3.2 in the Height box. Notice that the file size drops from 476K to 155K.

5 Click OK to resize the image.

With the art at the right size, you're ready to add the top border and type. In order to make room for these elements, you need to increase the canvas size until it approximates the actual size of the final brochure cover—3.5 inches wide and 5.6 inches high.

To increase the canvas size:

1 Choose Canvas Size from the Image menu. In the Canvas Size dialog box, enter 3.5 in the Width box and 5.6 in the Height box, click the center square in the placement box, then click OK to add the canvas at the top of the image.

2 Use the rectangular marquee to select the art, then drag the art down until the black border at the top of the art is aligned with the 2-1/2-inch marker on the ruler.

PAINTING WITH A PATTERN

Creating the top border begins with making a selection. Since you know the exact size you want the selection to be, you will use a fixed marquee to select the area.

In Lesson 2, you used the rubber stamp tool with the aligned options to duplicate areas within an image. In Lessons 2 and 3, you defined a pattern and then filled an area with that pattern. Now you're ready to combine these procedures by using the rubber stamp tool to duplicate a pattern in a selection.

To create the top border:

1 Use the Fixed Size option in the Rectangular Marquee Options dialog box to create a marquee with a Width of 190 and a Height of 30.

2 Click the white area in the window to make the marquee appear, then hold down the Control and Alt keys and drag the marquee up to the top edge of the image.

3 Use the rulers to center the marquee in the window.

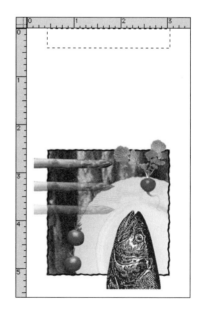

4 Open the WAVES.EPS file in the LESSON5 directory and click OK to accept the ESP Rasterizer default settings.

Don't worry if the screen turns gray; the color will return when you select another window.

5 Select the entire image, then choose Define Pattern from the Edit menu to copy the selection into the pattern buffer.

6 Close the WAVES.EPS file.

7 Double-click the rubber stamp tool to display the Rubber Stamp Options dialog box, and choose Pattern (aligned) from the Option pop-up menu.

8 Choose the far-right brush (the largest brush with hard edges) in the top row of the Brushes palette.

9 Starting from the left side of the selected marquee, paint the pattern with the rubber stamp tool (you'll probably need two passes to fill the selection).

FILLING A PATTERN WITH A GRADIENT

As you might remember from Lessons 2 and 4, a gradient fill displays a gradual transition from the foreground to the background color. You can create an interesting effect when you use gradient fills with a pattern.

To fill the pattern:

1 If you changed the foreground color, use the eyedropper to reset it by sampling the dark purple from along the back of the fish.

2 Copy the border selection to the Clipboard and then paste the selection back over itself.

You will need a pasted selection in order to use the composite controls to make the wave show through the fill.

3 Click the gradient tool and make sure the Opacity in the Brushes palette is set to 100 percent.

4 Place the crosshair for the starting point at the center of the bottom edge of the border.

5 Drag up to the top of the window.

Don't panic, your waves are still there! Currently the gradient overlays the selection. Notice that the gradient begins with the foreground color at the point that you click and ends with the background color at the end of the line you drag.

6 Choose Composite Controls from the Edit menu, then set the Opacity to 80 percent and choose Darken from the Mode pop-up menu.

7 Deselect the selection.

This allows the waves to show through the gradient.

8 Save the file as COVER6.PSD.

EDITING TYPE IN A CHANNEL

To complete this project, you'll add the brochure title. Before pasting in the type, you will adjust the spacing of individual characters by editing the type in a channel. Editing type in a channel allows you to make changes without affecting the background in the final image. For example, if you had a patterned background and attempted to move type in an image, the background would also move.

To create the type:

1 Sample the dark red from the edge of the radish for the new foreground color.

2 Click the type tool and make sure the Opacity in the Brushes palette is set to 100 percent.

3 Click the insertion point about half an inch below the border to display the Type Tool dialog box.

4 Choose Times from the Font pop-up menu.

5 Set the type size to 36 points, the Spacing to 1, the Leading to 0, and make sure the Left alignment option is selected.

6 Type **Eating for**, press the Return key, type **Your Health**, then click OK.

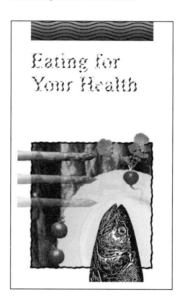

7 Choose Save Selection from the Select menu to save the type in channel #4.

To edit the type:

1 Click #4 in the Channels palette to display the type.

2 Click outside the type or choose None to deselect the type.

3 Choose Map from the Image menu and Invert from the submenu (or press Control+I).

The Invert command creates a negative of the image. Seeing the type as black against a white background will make it easier to edit, since you will be using the black marquee to isolate parts of the type.

4 Set the rectangular marquee tool shape to Normal.

5 Zoom in on the *Y* in *Your.*

6 Use the lasso tool to select the *Y,* then click the right arrow key twice to move the *Y* two pixels to the right.

The letter spacing of the *Y* is rather wide; moving it to the right improves the look of the type.

7 Use the rectangular marquee to select the top line of type, and press the right arrow key to move the type until it is centered over the second line of type.

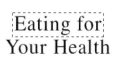

8 Zoom out and select the entire image, then choose Map from the Image menu and Invert from the submenu again.

This returns the channel to its original positive setting.

PASTING TYPE INTO AN IMAGE

Your last task for this project is to paste the type into the brochure cover.

To paste the type:

1 Click RGB in the Channels palette to return to the composite view.

2 Deselect the original type.

3 Use the rectangular marquee to select the type, then choose Cut from the Edit menu (or press Control+X) to delete the selection.

You need to delete the selection so that you won't have duplicate type when you load the edited type from channel #4 into the image.

4 Load the type selection stored in channel #4.

5 Fill the type with the foreground color. Be sure the Opacity is still 100 percent, and reset the fill mode to Normal, then click OK.

6 Use the arrow keys if you need to position the type.

7 Deselect the type, then save the file.

8 If you want to, you can print the image.

Eating for
Your Health

9 Close the files.

You should be proud! Not only have you created a very sophisticated piece of art, you've also learned a great deal about Adobe Photoshop in the last few hours. In the next lesson, you'll take some time to review what you've learned in Lessons 4 and 5.

LE MONDE

B

Gourmet Visions

LESSON 6: REVIEW PROJECT—WINE LABEL

This lesson gives you a chance to practice the commands and techniques you learned in the fourth and fifth lessons of *Classroom in a Book*.

The step-by-step instructions in this lesson provide all the information you need to complete the project; however, detailed explanations of procedures are not included. If you find that you want more precise instructions, or can't remember how to do something, refer back to Lessons 4 and 5. It should take you about 45 minutes to complete this lesson.

In this lesson, you'll create a wine label for a new vineyard whose wines are going to be stocked by Gourmet Visions markets. As you create the label, you'll combine the selection, masking, and manipulation techniques you already know in a new and interesting way. There are three source files for this lesson—a line drawing, a star graphic, and a file containing saved text.

Source file (STAR.PSD)

Source file (GRAPES.PSD)

Source file (LTYPE.PSD)

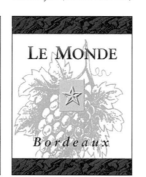
Ending image (WLABEL.PSD)

In this lesson, feel free to experiment with placement and pasting settings. Use the final image as a guide, but don't feel you must reproduce the label exactly. These review lessons are your opportunity to explore the features of Adobe Photoshop.

BEGINNING THIS LESSON

Again, in this lesson, you will have two images open on the screen: the file you begin with and the final version of the image.

To begin this lesson:

1 Open the WLABEL.PSD file in the LESSON6 directory, zoom out to reduce the image, resize the window, then drag the window to the upper-right corner of your screen.

2 Make sure the Colors, Paths, Info, and Channels palettes are open. Collapse the palettes and line them up on the right side of your screen below the WLABEL.PSD file.

3 Create a new RGB Color file that is 4.3 inches wide and 5.6 inches high with a resolution of 72. Be sure the units of measurement in the New dialog box are set to inches.

4 Turn on the rulers in the untitled window and save this file in your Projects directory as LABEL1.PSD.

5 Click the default colors icon to return to the default background and foreground colors.

DEFINING THE PATTERN

The first step in creating this label is to define the pattern you'll use for the top and bottom borders.

To define the pattern:

1 Open the GRAPES.PSD file in the LESSON6 directory and turn on the rulers in this window.

You will use this file in two different ways during this lesson. First, you'll select part of the grapes to use as the basis of your pattern. Later, you'll copy the entire bunch of grapes to serve as the main design element in the label.

2 Use the rectangular marquee to select a half-inch square area near the top of the grapes.

Since this selection does not have to be precise, you can use the normal marquee setting with the rectangular marquee tool.

3 Choose Define Pattern from the Edit menu.

MAKING A FIXED-SIZE SELECTION

You're going to use a fixed marquee to define the selection for the top border. You want the marquee to be exactly as wide as the image.

To select the border area:

1 Activate the LABEL1.PSD file.

2 Hold down the Alt key, click the page preview box to display the size preview box, and note the image width in pixels (310).

3 Click the Fixed Size option in the Rectangular Marquee Options dialog box and enter a Width of 310 and a Height of 46.

4 Click anywhere in the image to display the marquee, hold down the Control and Alt keys, and drag the marquee to the top edge of the window.

PAINTING WITH THE RUBBER STAMP TOOL

Now you're ready to paint the border using the pattern that's currently stored in the pattern buffer.

To paint the selection:

1 Choose the Pattern (aligned) option in the Rubber Stamp Options dialog box.

2 Choose any hard-edged brush from the Brushes palette and paint with the pattern.

CREATING A MARBLE EFFECT

To distort the grapes and produce the marble-like effect in the border, you're going to apply a filter to the selection.

To apply the filter:

1 Choose Distort from the Filter menu and Wave from the submenu. The Wave dialog box appears.

2 Enter 7 for the Number of Generators option and change the Type to Triangle, then click OK.

The pattern takes on a marble-like texture. If you want to experiment with the other settings in the Wave dialog box, go ahead and do it now. You can also try applying the same filter setting more than once to see how the selection changes.

ADDING COLOR TO A PATTERN

Now you're ready to make the border dark green.

To fill the pattern:

1 Set the R slider in the Colors palette to 0, set the G slider to about 84, and set the B slider to about 42 to select the foreground color.

2 In the Fill dialog box, select the Foreground option, set the Opacity to 100 percent, and choose the Darken mode to fill the pattern.

DUPLICATING A SELECTION

You could use the Copy and Paste commands to create the bottom border. Adobe Photoshop, however, provides a faster way to duplicate a selection by dragging.

To duplicate the selection:

1 Double-click the rectangular marquee tool, and set the option to Normal.

2 Choose Copy from the Edit menu.

3 Choose Paste from the Edit menu.

4 Drag the selection to the bottom of the image, press the shift key, then release the keys.

A copy of the selection moves as you drag.

5 Save the file as LABEL2.PSD.

CLEANING UP A SCANNED IMAGE

You may have noticed the smudges around the cluster of grapes in the GRAPES.PSD file. These types of imperfections are frequently found on scanned images. You're going to use Quick Mask mode to clean up these areas before pasting the bunch of grapes into your LABEL2.PSD file.

To edit the scanning marks:

1 Activate the GRAPES.PSD file.

2 Set the tolerance for the magic wand tool to 32, then click to select the white background area.

Notice that neither the grapes nor the smudged areas are part of the selection (which you will invert before you copy and paste). You need to add the smudged areas to the selection.

3 Click the Quick Mask control in the toolbox.

All the protected areas appear in light green (the color you set for the mask when you used it in Lesson 4). If someone has been using the program, the selected areas might be another color or may appear in the default red color. If the background (instead of the grapes) is selected, open the Quick Mask dialog box and select the Color Indicates Masked Areas option.

4 Make sure the default background and foreground colors are set, then use the eraser to remove the color over the smudged areas.

Since the color indicates a masked area, you are removing these areas from the mask.

5 Click the Standard Mode control (to the left of the Quick Mask mode control in the toolbox).

6 Inverse the selection.

Only the grape cluster is included in the selection. For safety's sake, you might want to save this selection before closing the file. If you do save the selection, save this file as GRAPES1.PSD before closing it.

7 Copy the selection to the Clipboard and close the file. Don't save your changes unless you are saving under the new name.

PASTING INTO A SELECTED AREA

With the selection on the Clipboard, you're ready to paste it into the LABEL2.PSD file.

To paste into a selected area:

1 Activate the LABEL2.PSD file.

2 Use the magic wand to select the center white area of the image.

3 Choose Paste Into from the Edit menu.

You might be wondering why you used the Paste Into command in this case. Why not just paste the selection in the ordinary way since the selection is placed in the center of the file and all of it is visible? You used Paste Into because you're going to increase the size of the selection, and you want the borders to cover part of this larger selection in the final image.

4 Make sure the Info palette is visible.

5 Choose Rotate from the Image menu and Free from the submenu.

Notice that an angle measurement is added to the Info palette (similar to the percentages that appear when you're scaling a selection).

6 Drag the upper-right handle until the Info palette reads about 30 degrees.

7 Click with the gavel icon to confirm the rotation.

8 Drag the selection down so that the bottom four or five grapes are hidden. The tip of the stem should be about 2-1/2 inches from the left edge of the window, and about 1-1/2 inches from the top.

SCALING UP A SELECTION

To achieve the correct balance in the final wine label, you need to increase the size of the selection slightly.

To scale up the selection:

1 Choose Effects from the Image menu and Scale from the submenu.

2 Hold down the Shift key to constrain the proportions, then drag the upper-right handle on a diagonal off the window until the measurement in the Info palette reads about 112 percent.

3 Click with the gavel icon to confirm the scaling.

4 Drag or use the arrow keys to center the image horizontally and position the tip of the stem about a quarter inch from the top border.

5 Save the file.

FILLING THE DARK AREAS OF A SELECTION

As a final step in modifying the grapes, you're going to fill the black areas in the selection with color.

To fill the grapes:

1 Sample a green area of the grapes in the WLABEL.PSD image.

2 Fine-tune the color by setting the sliders in the Colors palette to read R equal to 183, G equal to 193, and B equal to 125.

3 Add this color to the Colors palette.

4 Fill the grapes using an Opacity of 100 percent and the Lighten mode.

5 Deselect to see the final effect.

CENTERING A SELECTION

Now you're ready to add the star seal to the label. To do this you will first make a solid-colored selection in the center of the label, and then copy a star selection from another file into this image.

To center a selection:

1 Set the rectangular marquee to a fixed size of 64 pixels wide by 80 pixels high.

2 Use the *X* and *Y* coordinates in the Info palette to set the crosshair for the marquee in the center of the window. The *X* value should be about 2.2 and the *Y* value should be about 2.8.

3 Hold down the Alt key as you click to display the marquee.

As you may remember, holding down the Alt key starts a marquee from the center rather than from an edge.

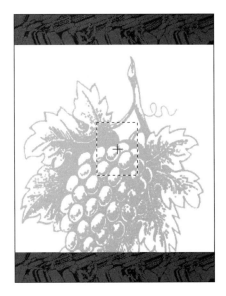

TYPING IN VALUES FOR A COLOR

In most cases, you have been setting a foreground color by sampling a color from an open window or changing the sliders in the Colors palette.

In Lesson 2, you also learned how to choose a color from the Color Picker. When you need to be very precise in setting color values (for example, when you are doing four-color separation), you can also type color values into the Color Picker. This is sometimes easier than trying to move the Colors palette sliders to an exact location.

To type the numerical values for a color:

1 Click the foreground color selection box in the toolbox to display the Color Picker.

The RGB color-value text boxes are located to the right of the bottom half of the color slider.

2 Click the R button, click the R text box, and type in 243. Click the G button, click the G text box, and type 203. Click the B button, click the B text box, and type 14.

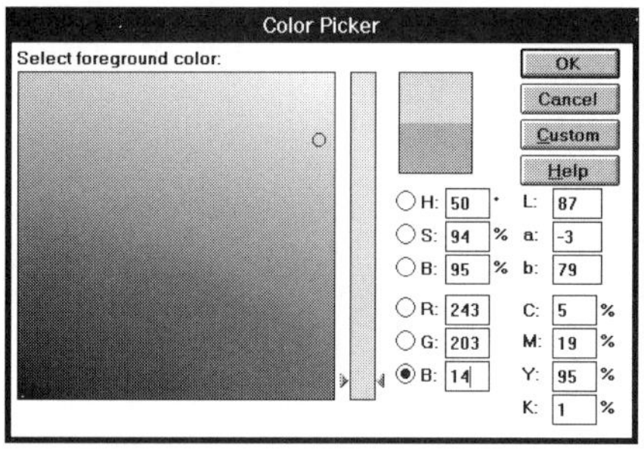

The colors will fluctuate widely as you are entering the values. When you've finished typing, the new foreground color will appear in the top of the color selection box to the right of the color slider.

3 Click OK to close the Color Picker.

4 Fill the selection using an Opacity setting of 100 percent and the Normal mode.

5 Save the file as Label3.PSD.

SAVING A PATH AS A SELECTION

The first step in creating the seal is to trace the star using the pen tool.

To copy the star:

1 Open the STAR.PSD file in the LESSON6 directory, zoom in twice, then resize the window (using the resize box in the upper-right corner) so you can see the entire star.

2 Use the pen tool to select the star shape.

3 Make the path into a selection.

4 Use the arrow point in the Paths palette to click anywhere outside the path to deselect the path (the selection will still have a marquee around it).

5 Save this file as STAR1.PSD in the Projects directory to associate the saved selection with the file.

6 Copy the selection to the Clipboard, then close the STAR1.PSD file (it's OK to close it with an unsaved path).

7 Paste the selection into the LABEL3.PSD file.

8 If necessary, center the star in the seal.

9 Use the Composite Controls dialog box to dim the star by setting the Opacity to 80 percent, and fill only the light areas by choosing the Darken mode.

10 Save the file.

EMBOSSING THE SELECTION

To create the *raised* effect on the seal, you're going to apply the Emboss filter. The Emboss filter suppresses the color within the selection and traces the outside of the selection with black.

To emboss the seal:

1 Use the rectangular marquee tool to select the yellow area in the image.

Unless you've changed it, the fixed marquee should still be set, and you can simply drag it over the square to make the selection.

2 Choose Stylize from the Filter menu and Emboss from the submenu. The Emboss dialog box appears.

3 If necessary, set the options to their default values of an Angle of 135 degrees, a Height of 3 pixels, and an Amount of 100 percent.

The *Adobe Photoshop User Guide* provides a detailed discussion of these options (as well as all the options in the other filter dialog boxes).

4 Click OK to apply the filter.

It's all right that the selection turns gray! The Emboss filter removes the color, but you'll put it back in a moment.

REAPPLYING COLOR TO AN EMBOSSED SELECTION

You will use the Colorize option that you learned about in Lesson 5 to return the color to the seal.

To return the color to the selection:

1 Choose Adjust from the Image menu and Hue/Saturation from the submenu.

2 Click the Colorize option in the dialog box and set the Hue to 52, the Saturation to 90, and the Lightness to 0.

3 Save the file as LABEL4.PSD.

EDITING THE LABEL TYPE

For the finishing touch, you're going to add the type to the wine label. This type, which uses the Palatino font, is provided in a separate file. You will add a gradient to the type before copying it to the wine label.

To add and edit the type:

1 Open the LTYPE.PSD file in the LESSON6 directory.

2 Select the entire image and copy it to the Clipboard.

You will need to paste the contents of the selection into the channel for editing.

3 Save the entire image as a selection.

4 Click #4 in the Channels palette to display the channel.

Are you surprised that the image is blank? If so, remember that to save the contents of a selection you copy it to the Clipboard; the Save Selection command saves only the shape of the selection border.

5 Choose Paste to make the text appear in the channel.

6 Return to the composite RGB view, and load the selection.

Everything but the text is selected.

7 Inverse the selection.

This is an easy way to get type selected without having to select each individual letter.

L E   M O N D E

Bordeaux

ADDING A GRADIENT FILL TO TEXT

Now that the type is selected, you're ready to add the gradient fill to the type.

To fill the type:

1 Choose a dark purple from the Colors palette or mix your own color to select a new foreground color.

2 Click the gradient tool and place the crosshair between the *M* and the *o* in *Monde*.

3 Drag straight up about halfway to the top of the window.

The type is filled with the color. Notice that the *Bordeaux* text is filled with the solid purple. When you create a gradient, the area in the image before the location where you click is filled with the foreground color. Notice also that there is no pure white in the *Le Monde* text. This is because the background color for a fill begins where you end the line you drag. In this case, the pure background color is halfway to the top of the window.

4 Copy the selection and paste it into the LABEL4.PSD file.

5 Deselect to see the finished label and save the file.

6 Print the file if you want to, then close the files.

Nice going! You should really feel that you're getting to be an experienced Adobe Photoshop user by now. With the completion of this lesson, you've accomplished a great deal and have a real understanding of Adobe Photoshop's editing capabilities.

The remaining lessons in *Classroom in a Book* move into the more sophisticated features of Adobe Photoshop, including color correction, resolution and resizing, mode conversion, and creating color separations.

LE MONDE

B

Gourmet Visions

Lesson

7

LESSON 7: UNDERSTANDING COLOR

This lesson discusses the Adobe Photoshop features that let you alter and manipulate color in images. You're already familiar with quite a few color manipulation tools from previous lessons. For example, you've used the Fill command to replace color in a selection, the Hue/Saturation command to change color and intensity, and the paste controls to determine how two colors blend during compositing.

In this lesson, you'll learn about the Adobe Photoshop tools designed for *color correction*. Just as there are varying levels of color adjustments you'll need to make, there are a variety of controls that offer you progressively more precise color control.

The lesson begins with a brief introduction to color theory and color models as they are used in Adobe Photoshop. You will then color-correct two images. It should take you about two hours to complete this lesson.

In this lesson, you'll learn how to do the following:

- measure color in a number of models

- display images with different palettes

- correct the color of an image using the Variations command

- use a histogram to measure tonal ranges

- adjust color levels in an image

- adjust curves in an image

- use the Info palette to preview color changes

- color-correct a selection

- use the dodge/burn and blur/sharpen tools

- sharpen detail in an image

- color-correct an individual channel

At the end of this lesson you'll have two color-corrected images of the chef, all ready to be used in the Gourmet Visions annual report. The following illustrations show the two images you'll work with in this lesson.

Ending image (PORTRAIT.PSD)   *Ending image (CHEF.PSD)*

During the review of color theory, you will want to have the Colors palette open on the screen. You can close any other palettes.

LOOKING AT COLOR MODELS

A color model is a method for displaying and measuring color. The three main models used in Adobe Photoshop are the RGB model for display, the CMYK model for printing, and the Lab model for both display and printing.

RGB

As you learned in Lesson 1, the human eye perceives color according to the wavelength of the light that reaches it. Light containing the full color spectrum is perceived as white. When no light is present, the eye perceives black.

All monitors display color using a mixture of the primary additive colors of red, green, and blue.

To see an example of additive color:

1 Open the ADDCOLOR.PSD file in the LESSON7 directory.

Combining these primary additive colors produces a large percentage of the visible spectrum. You can see that combining red and green produces yellow, combining green and blue produces cyan, and combining blue and red produces magenta. The result of combining all three colors is white (as shown in the center of the wheel).

Measuring RGB color

In RGB color, various brightness values of red, green, and blue light combine to form the colors on the screen. When you're working in Adobe Photoshop's RGB *mode,* you control the range of colors by varying the intensities of the individual RGB components. Up until now, you've been working in the RGB mode. For example, when you selected or modified a color using the sliders in the Colors palette or the values in the Color Picker, you adjusted the red, green, and blue values to display a particular color.

For RGB color images, Adobe Photoshop assigns an intensity value to each pixel ranging from 0 (black) to 255 (white) for each of the RGB components. To see how this works in practice, you're going to experiment using the Colors palette.

To display the RGB components of a color:

1 Open the Colors palette and click the red swatch at the far left in the top row.

Notice that the color values next to the sliders move to an R value of 255, and G and B values of 0. This indicates that this color contains only a red component; there is no green or blue in this color.

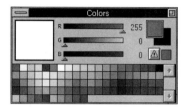

2 Drag the R slider all the way to the left until it reads 0.

The resulting color is black, since none of the components has any value.

3 Click the green swatch (the third swatch from the left) in the top row of the Colors palette.

This pure green produces values of 0 for the R and B components and 255 for the G component.

4 Slide the R slider to the right until it reads 255.

When both the R and G sliders read 255, the resulting color is yellow.

5 Drag the B slider to the right until it reads 255.

When all three sliders read 255, the resulting color is pure white.

6 Drag all three sliders to the center until their values are about 127.

You can see that when all three components have the same value, the resulting mixture is a gray color.

7 Use the sliders to create magenta and cyan.

You can use the ADDCOLOR.PSD file as a guide. As you move the sliders, watch how the proportions of each component determine the resulting color.

8 Close the ADDCOLOR.PSD file.

CMYK

In Lesson 1 you also learned that the color you see on a printed page is a result of color being absorbed, or subtracted, by the inks on the page. As white light strikes translucent inks, a portion of the color spectrum is absorbed; color that is not absorbed is reflected back to the observer.

To see an example of subtractive color:

1 Open the SUBCOLOR.PSD file in the LESSON7 directory.

In theory, a mixture of the primary subtractive colors (or *process colors*) of cyan, magenta, and yellow (CMY) should produce black (K). Because of ink impurities, however, these three inks produce a muddy brown, and more black must be added to produce a pure black.

Measuring CMYK color

When you're working in CMYK mode, Adobe Photoshop assigns each pixel a percentage value for each of the process inks. The lightest colors are assigned smaller percentages; darker inks have higher percentages. You can read the value for any color in CMYK percentages in the Colors palette.

Important: Although you can set color values for CMYK colors in Adobe Photoshop, the actual display of the color on your screen is in RGB color (your monitor can only display using additive colors).

To display the CMYK components of a color:

1 Choose CMYK Color from the Colors palette pop-up menu.

Adobe Photoshop lets you set color values in a number of color-model systems. For the CMYK model, an additional slider appears and the values for the current color are given as percentages. See the *Adobe Photoshop User Guide* for information on the other color models in the pop-up menu (the Lab Color option is explained in the next section).

2 Click the white swatch in the top row of the Colors palette (the seventh swatch from the left).

The sliders move all the way to the left, since in CMYK values pure white contains 0 percent of the process colors (that is, you see white since all the color is reflected back to your eye).

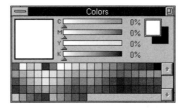

3 Slide the cyan and yellow sliders all the way to the right, until they read 100 percent.

Combining 100 percent of cyan and 100 percent of yellow produces green.

4 Slowly slide the black slider to the right and watch how adding more black changes the color.

5 Experiment with the sliders to see if you can produce orange. As you move the sliders, watch how the various combinations of percentages produce different colors.

6 Close the SUBCOLOR.PSD file.

Out-of-gamut colors

The *gamut* of a color system is the range of colors that can be displayed or printed.

To see the overlay of gamuts:

1 Open the GAMUT.PSD file in the LESSON7 directory.

Each of the color models has a different color gamut. When colors that cannot be printed are displayed on the screen (that is, they are outside the CMYK gamut), an alert triangle with an exclamation mark appears in the Colors palette (and in the Color Picker and Info palette). The GAMUT.PSD file is not a realistic measurement for color. It is just a visual representation of the term gamut.

2 Look at the Gamut illustration to get a feel for the color ranges in the various color models.

3 Close the GAMUT.PSD file.

To display an out-of-gamut color:

1 Choose RGB Color from the Colors palette pop-up menu to display the colors in the RGB model.

2 Click the yellow swatch in the top row of the Colors palette.

This yellow is out of the CMYK gamut, so the triangle appears below the color selection boxes. The closest CMYK color equivalent appears next to the triangle.

3 Click the triangle.

Adobe Photoshop automatically selects the printable color closest to the color you selected.

The range of printable colors depends on your output device. The availability of printable colors is determined by the printing values you enter in the Printing Inks Setup box. See Lesson 11 for more information on colors and printing.

Lab

L*a*b* is a color model developed by the Centre Internationale d'Eclairage (CIE), an international organization that established specifications for measuring color in 1931. These specifications are the internationally accepted standard for all color-imetric measurements. The Lab model, like other CIE color models, defines color values mathematically, in a way that is device-independent. This means that Lab colors do not vary with different, properly calibrated monitors or printers.

The Lab gamut encompasses both the RGB and CMYK gamuts; it is a standardized color model that comprises all colors. Using Lab color gives you a way to create consistent color documents regardless of the device used to create or print the file.

To see a representation of the Lab model:

1 Open the LABMODEL.PSD file in the LESSON7 directory.

Lab images consist of a luminance, or lightness, component (*L*) and two chromatic components: the *a* component, which ranges from green to magenta, and the *b* component, which ranges from blue to yellow.

2 Choose Lab Color from the Mode menu.

To display the Lab components of a color:

1 Choose Lab Color from the Colors palette pop-up menu.

Three sliders appear, one for each of the Lab components. Lab values can range from −120 (on the far left) to +120 (on the far right).

2 Click the blue swatch in the top row of the Colors palette (the fifth swatch from the left).

3 Drag the *L* slider to the right until it reads 60 to increase the color's luminance.

Because Lab color lets you adjust lightness separately from the color values, it can be a useful editing tool.

4 Drag the *a* slider to the left until it reads –79 to add green and produce an aqua color.

5 Drag the *b* slider to the right until it reads 0 to remove blue and produce a turquoise color.

6 Pick a new color and drag the sliders around to see how Lab colors are formed.

7 Close the LABMODEL.PSD file.

SELECTING A PALETTE FOR THE COLOR DISPLAY

Each image type in Adobe Photoshop uses a different *color lookup table*, or *color palette*, to store the colors used in the image. To optimize the display for each image, the program stores a different palette for each open file (based on the colors in the image), and displays the active document using its associated palette. Adobe Photoshop uses a technique called *dithering* to simulate the display of colors that are not in the current color palette.

Using the document's individual palette is the preferred method of display because it shows you the colors most accurately. Keep in mind, however, that using the file's individual palette can make the colors in inactive documents look less accurate.

You can choose to display all open documents using the System color palette (rather than the document's individual palette) by clicking the Use System Palette option in the General Preferences dialog box. Choosing the System palette can make the display of colors in the active document less accurate. See the *Adobe Photoshop User Guide* for more information on display palettes and dithering options.

MAKING COLOR CORRECTIONS

Color correction allows you to address differences between the original or scanned image and the image as it appears on the screen or in print. Color correction also lets you compensate for some common problems in four-color reproduction, such as the varying contrast between paper and ink and the inability of process inks to match their theoretical performance. In order for your color corrections to be accurate for printing, your system must be calibrated correctly. See Lesson 11 and the *Adobe Photoshop User Guide* for more information on calibrating your system and printing four-color separations.

BEGINNING THIS LESSON

Now you are ready to put some of this theory to work. The first image you'll color-correct is a portrait of a chef.

Important: *Before doing any of the tasks in this lesson, be sure your monitor has been calibrated following the instructions in Lesson 1. If the monitor is not calibrated correctly, you will get some very different results when you color-correct the images.*

Note: *Because of differences in hardware and work environments, some of the corrected files you open from the LESSON7 directory might not be precisely color-corrected for your system. As you work through the lesson, adjust the color so that the file you're working on matches the color in the final image as it appears on your screen, even if that image is a bit out of balance. The idea is for you to understand the controls and procedures for making color corrections, not to produce a perfectly color-corrected image.*

TIP: YOU CAN ALSO UNDO ANY CHANGES YOU'VE MADE IN THE VARIATIONS DIALOG BOX BY PRESSING THE ALT KEY AND CLICKING THE RESET BUTTON (THE CANCEL BUTTON CHANGES TO RESET WHEN YOU HOLD DOWN THE ALT KEY).

To begin the lesson:

1 Open the CPORTRAI.PSD file in the LESSON7 directory, zoom out to reduce the image, resize the window, then drag the window to the upper-right corner of your screen.

2 Open the PORTRAIT.PSD file in the LESSON7 directory.

3 Make sure the Colors, Info, and Brushes palettes are open. You won't need the Channels palette or the Paths palette for this lesson.

Since you don't need any palettes for the first part of this lesson, you can collapse the open palettes if you want to.

USING THE VARIATIONS COMMAND

The first color correction you're going to make is to adjust the overall color in this portrait. Currently, this image is too light, has too little contrast, and has an unappealing overall blue/magenta cast. This kind of imbalance might result from a poor exposure setting or the use of an incorrect filter or film type when the photograph was shot. Some of these problems could also have been introduced during the scanning process. You're going to correct this image using the Variations command.

Using the Variations command is a quick and easy way to visually adjust the color balance, contrast, and saturation in an image or selection.

To use the Variations command:

1 Choose Adjust from the Image menu and Variations from the submenu. The Variations dialog box appears.

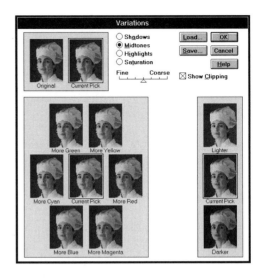

The two thumbnails at the top of the dialog box show you the Original selection and the Current Pick (in this case, they are the same since you haven't made any corrections yet). As you change the settings, the Current Pick shows you the latest version of the corrected image. To color-correct the image, you simply click the thumbnail that looks the closest to the effect you're trying to achieve.

The thumbnails in the bottom-left section let you adjust color balance. The colors are arranged according to their positions on the color wheel; yellow is at 45 degrees, red is at 90 degrees, and so on.

2 Click the More Red thumbnail.

The color balance from the More Red thumbnail becomes the new Current Pick in the center of this section (it's also the new Current Pick at the top of the dialog box). Since you are adjusting color balance, each time you make a choice, all of the thumbnails change. Was this effect too minor for you to see?

3 Click More Red again.

Repeatedly clicking a thumbnail incrementally adjusts the image. Look at the top of the dialog box to compare the Original selection with the Current Pick. You can see a definite change in the image. Unfortunately, this is not the direction you want to go in.

4 Click the Original thumbnail in the upper-left corner of the dialog box to return to your image's original color.

Adjusting the midtones

The Variations command lets you focus the color correction on the dark areas (Shadows), the middle tones (Midtones), or the light areas (Highlights) of the image. In general, the order in which you make color corrections depends on what is wrong with the image. Because this image has a strong color cast, you will begin by correcting the color in the midtones and then adjust the skin tones.

To adjust midtones:

1 Select the Midtones option.

The lower-right section of the Variations dialog box lets you make the image lighter or darker. The Current Pick is in the middle of this section.

2 Click Darker.

Again, all the thumbnails change to show the adjustment. Making the image darker removes its washed-out look.

3 In the left section, click More Green to remove the magenta cast from the image.

With less magenta, the skin tones begin to improve. Since green and magenta are complementary colors, adding more green decreases the magenta in the image.

4 Click More Yellow to remove the blue cast.

Blue and yellow are also complementary colors. Now the image is really coming to life.

Adjusting the highlights and shadows

To increase the contrast in the image, you darken the shadows and lighten the highlights.

To adjust the contrast:

1 Select the Shadows option.

2 Drag the Fine/Coarse slider one notch to the right.

The Fine/Coarse slider determines the increment of change that each click of a thumbnail represents. Moving the slider to the right (toward Coarse) doubles the effect; moving it to the left (toward Fine) halves the effect.

3 Make sure the Show Clipping option is selected.

Clipping (or loss of color) occurs when an adjustment causes a color to exceed its maximum or minimum value. For example, if you increase the contrast too much, light grays are converted to white and dark grays are converted to black. Clipping can also occur when a color exceeds its maximum saturation. Clipped areas are shown in neon colors.

4 Click Darker.

The overall contrast of the image improves. Some of the thumbnails show areas where clipping would occur.

5 Select the Highlights option.

6 Click Lighter.

This final adjustment makes the whites stand out crisp and clear.

7 Click OK to apply the corrections to the image.

With just a few simple clicks, you've turned an unacceptable image into a dynamically balanced portrait. If you want to compare your beginning and ending images, choose Undo and Redo from the Edit menu.

8 Save this file as PORT1.PSD in the Projects directory.

9 Close both files.

DEVISING A STRATEGY FOR PRECISE COLOR CORRECTION

Using the Variations command is a quick and intuitive way to color-correct an image. Sometimes, however, an image needs more precise adjustments than can be made using the Variations command. Adobe Photoshop offers several additional color-correction tools to help you make more exact color adjustments.

The key to good color reproduction is to produce an image with proper *tonal balance* (correct brightness, saturation, contrast, and density range) and no color deficiencies. Making your color corrections in a specific order can help you achieve this goal.

Here's a suggested strategy for color correction:

1 Set the highlight (white) and shadow (black) points in the image.

2 Make adjustments to the middle tones.

3 Correct for overall color imbalance (such as color cast in skin tones or a green cast from fluorescent lighting).

4 Make selective color corrections. For example, you might want to make a sky bluer or take some yellow out of a landscape of trees.

5 Apply the Unsharp Mask filter.

Don't worry if none of this makes much sense to you right now. You'll understand it all by the time you finish this lesson. Use this strategy as a guide later, when you're working on your own color-correction projects.

PERFORMING PRECISE COLOR CORRECTION

Now you're going to color-correct another image of the chef using this strategy. Once again, you will open a file to refer to as you make the color corrections.

To open the files:

1 Open the CCHEF.PSD file in the LESSON7 directory, zoom out to reduce the image, resize the window, then drag the window to the upper-right corner of your screen.

2 Open the CHEF.PSD file in the LESSON7 directory.

Like the earlier portrait, this image appears flat, with little contrast and a decided color cast—in this case, an overall yellow tone.

3 Make sure the CHEF.PSD window is active.

DETERMINING THE TONAL RANGE IN AN IMAGE

A *histogram* is a graphic representation of tonal range (brightness and darkness levels) in an image. It plots the number of pixels at each level.

The distribution of pixels can dramatically affect the appearance of an image. If a wide range of levels is used to depict an uninteresting area of the image (such as a dark background or bright highlight), only a narrow range of levels is available for the focus of interest (usually the midtone areas in the image). You use a histogram to check for optimum brightness and contrast as you make color corrections.

To display the histogram:

1 Choose Histogram from the Image menu. The Histogram dialog box appears.

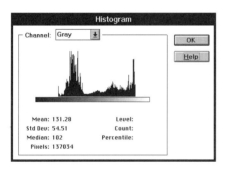

The *x*-axis of the histogram shows the color values of the pixels from the darkest (0) at the far left to the brightest (255) at the far right. The *y*-axis represents the number of pixels with that value. Statistical information about the pixels appears in the lower left of the dialog box.

You can see that there are very few pixels in the shadow and highlight areas of this histogram, which reflects the visual flatness of this image.

2 Move the pointer into the histogram area.

3 Click any spot where there are pixels in the histogram.

The values at the lower right of the dialog box change to display the level of the point (from 0 to 255), the total number of pixels at that point, and the percentage of pixels below that point. If you want the values for a range of pixels, drag the crosshair in the histogram.

4 Click OK to close the dialog box.

This histogram is for information only; you don't make any adjustments using the Histogram command.

5 For comparison, make the CCHEF.PSD window active and choose the Histogram command again.

You can see that the pixels in this image cover the entire range of values from light to dark as you would expect in a color-corrected image.

6 Close the Histogram dialog box and activate the CHEF.PSD window.

ADJUSTING COLOR WITH THE LEVELS COMMAND

Now that the histogram has given you an idea of the starting point for the tonal balance of this image, you're going to make corrections using the Levels command. Getting a good range of overall density levels is the main step in producing a good color image.

The Levels dialog box includes options that allow you to indicate the pixels in the image that you want to represent the darkest and brightest points (or the end points of the color-value scale). Setting the *black point* (shadow) and the *white point* (highlight) redistributes the pixels in the image and automatically produces a good overall tonal balance. You can also set a *neutral gray* point.

Before opening the Levels dialog box, you're going to use the eyedropper to find the darkest and lightest points. Remember, a pure black point has RGB values all equal to 0, and a pure white point has RGB values all equal to 255.

To find the darkest and lightest points:

1 Be sure you can see the Info palette, then click the eyedropper.

2 Move the eyedropper over the piece of hair in front of the chef's ear.

Locate the darkest point in the hair (the point closest to 0 for all values). The RGB values should be about 40 for R, 63 for G, and 28 for B. Make a note of this location.

3 Move the eyedropper around in the bright white area of the chef's smock to the left of the peppers.

Locate the lightest point in the smock (the point closest to 255 for all values). The RGB values should be about 210 for R, 227 for G, and 209 for B. Remember the location of this point.

Now you are ready to adjust the image.

To use the Levels command:

1 Choose Adjust from the Image menu and Levels from the submenu (or press Control+L). The Levels dialog box appears.

Here is the same histogram of the image, showing the compressed shadows and highlights.

2 Make sure the Preview option is selected, then drag the dialog box down so you can see the top portions of the image.

3 Click the black eyedropper in the Levels dialog box.

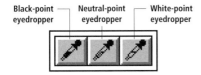

Black-point eyedropper — Neutral-point eyedropper — White-point eyedropper

4 Click the point that you earlier determined to be the darkest point in the image.

Clicking this dark point sets the value of this pixel to 0 (or black) and produces a darker image with more contrast. Notice that the histogram shifts to the left to show the change in pixel distribution. Although this improves the contrast, the image is too dark and the highlights are dull.

5 Click the white eyedropper in the Levels dialog box, then drag the dialog box to the right so you can see the chef's body.

6 Click the point that you earlier determined to be the brightest point in the image.

Setting this white point brings out the brightness of the chef's hat and smock and lightens the image. Notice that the histogram now shows a good overall range of pixel values and reflects the tonal balance of the corrected image.

In changing the white point, some of the tone in the white areas (highlights) has been lost. You need to decrease the contrast in the highlights to bring out some detail.

Decreasing contrast using the Levels command

The Output Levels slider in the Levels dialog box decreases the contrast in an image.

To decrease the contrast:

1 Drag the white triangle for the Output Levels (the one directly below the white end of the *gradation bar*) to the left, until the right text box above the gradation bar reads 239.

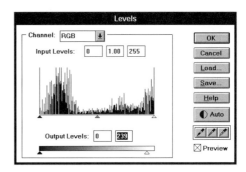

This tells Adobe Photoshop to take all the pixels with values between 239 and 255 and make their new value 239. Redistributing some highlight pixels produces a darker image with less contrast, so that the white areas take on more tone.

In the same way, dragging the black triangle for the Output Levels redistributes some shadow pixels and decreases contrast, producing a lighter image.

Increasing contrast using the Levels command

The Input Levels slider increases the contrast in an image. Although the contrast is good in this image, you're going to make the background slightly darker (that is, increase the contrast in the shadow areas).

To increase the contrast:

1 Drag the black triangle for the Input Levels (the one directly below the left edge of the *histogram*) to the right, until the left text box above the histogram reads 11.

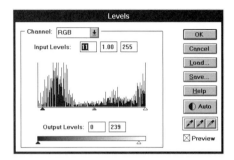

This tells Adobe Photoshop to take all the dark pixels with values between 0 and 11 and make their value 0. Moving the black triangle to the right redistributes the shadow pixels, producing a darker image with more contrast.

2 Click OK to apply the new settings.

3 Press Control+L to display the Levels dialog box again.

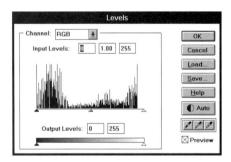

The histogram has changed to reflect the new distribution of pixels in the image. Notice that there are no pixels at the far right of the histogram, reflecting the removal of some highlight values. The left side of the histogram shows the bunching caused by the redistribution of the shadow pixels.

Adjusting midtones using the Levels command

The *gamma* triangle for the Input Levels controls the midtone pixels. Although you don't need to adjust the gamma in this image, take some time now to experiment with this control so you'll know how to adjust the midtones in your own images.

To adjust the midtones:

1 Drag the gamma triangle (the gray triangle under the middle of the Input Levels histogram) to the right, until the middle text box reads about 80.

The midtones in the image, especially those in the face, are darkened, while the highlights and shadows remain the same. In this case, however, this adjustment makes the midtones too dark.

2 Hold down the Alt key and click the Reset button to undo the gamma adjustment, then click Cancel to close the dialog box.

As in the Variations dialog box, holding down Alt changes the name of the Cancel button to Reset.

ADJUSTING COLOR WITH THE CURVES COMMAND

Like the Levels command, the Curves command lets you adjust the shadow, highlights, and midtones of an image. However, instead of making the adjustments using just three variables (highlights, shadows, and gamma), you can adjust any point along the gray levels curve for the image. Now you're going to color-correct this same image using the Curves command. To start with the same overexposed image, you must first undo the corrections you just made.

To use the Curves command:

1 Choose Revert from the File menu.

If you saved the file after making the color corrections, just reopen the CHEF.PSD file from the LESSON7 directory.

2 Choose Adjust from the Image menu and Curves from the submenu (or press Control+M). The Curves dialog box appears.

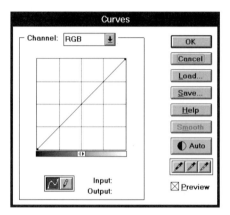

The *x*-axis of the graph represents the original brightness value of the pixels, from 0 to 255 (input levels); the *y*-axis represents the adjusted brightness values (output levels).

The grayscale along the bottom of the dialog box moves from black on the left (0) to white on the right (255). (If your Curves dialog box has the grayscale reversed—white is on the left—click the arrows in the bar under the graph.)

The lines across the graph indicate the *shadow tones* along the bottom border of the box, the *three-quarter tones* (three-quarters of the way between white and black), the *midtones*, the *quarter tones*, and the *highlight tones* along the top border.

3 Click the eyedropper tool in the toolbox and press down the mouse button as you move around in the darkest area of the image (the piece of hair in front of the chef's ear).

As you move the eyedropper, a circle appears on the graph in the Curves dialog box showing you the value of the pixel you're over in the image. The darkest area will appear closest to the lower-left corner of the graph.

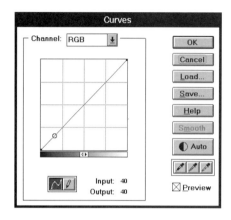

4 Use the eyedropper to locate the brightest point in the chef's smock (the circle will appear closest to the top-right corner of the graph for the brightest point).

5 Click the black eyedropper in the Curves dialog box, then click the darkest point to set the black point.

6 Click the white eyedropper in the Curves dialog box, then click the brightest point to set the white point.

Changing contrast using the Curves command

The line in the Curves graph shows the current relationship between the input values and the output values of the pixels. The diagonal line indicates a value of one to one—that is, every pixel has the same input and output value. To use the Curves dialog box, you click *control points* along this line and change the curve of the line by dragging up or down.

To change the image contrast:

1 Make sure the Preview option in the Curves dialog box is selected.

2 Move the crosshair along the diagonal line and stop at about the middle of the graph.

Watch the Input and Output levels at the bottom of the Curves dialog box. You want to position the crosshair on the line so that the Input and Output values both read about 126.

3 Drag the control point down and to the left, and watch how the image gets darker.

The Input level is now higher than the Output level, indicating that the pixel's value is moving toward black, or becoming darker.

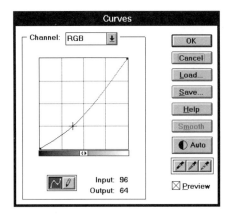

4 Click the same point on the line and drag up and to the left.

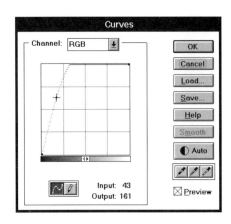

The Input level is now lower than the Output level, indicating that the pixel's value is moving toward white, or becoming lighter.

5 Click the control point and drag it off the graph to return to the original diagonal line.

Adjusting contrast using the Curves command

The first adjustment you made in the Levels dialog box was to reduce the contrast in the white areas. You then increased the contrast in the dark areas. You're going to drag the curve in this dialog box to make the same adjustments.

1 Click the square at the upper-right corner of the line and drag horizontal along the top edge of the graph, until the Input value reads about 239 and the Output value reads about 255.

If you don't see any Input or Output values, you probably have the pointer slightly outside the graph borders.

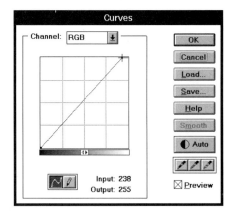

This redistributes the highlight pixels and decreases the contrast in the highlights.

2 Click the square at the bottom-left corner of the line and drag horizontally along the bottom border of the graph, until the Input value reads 11 and the Output value reads 0.

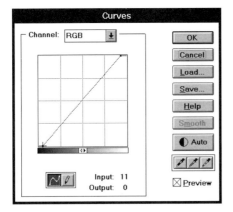

This redistributes the shadow pixels and increases the contrast in the dark areas.

3 Click the quarter tones area and drag down slightly and to the right to adjust the gamma tones.

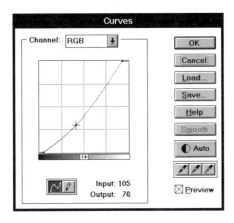

This should be only a slight adjustment. Experiment with this slider until the image looks correct on your screen.

The Levels and Curves dialog boxes also contain a neutral-gray eyedropper. You can use this eyedropper to set a starting point for correcting your middle tones and removing a color cast from the image.

4 Click OK to apply the settings.

USING THE INFO PALETTE AS A DENSITOMETER

A *densitometer* is a tool that reads the percentage (density) of black in a pixel. When you're making color corrections, you can use the Info palette as a densitometer to preview the changes in density before and after an adjustment. As you know, when you move the eyedropper over a pixel, that pixel's values appear in the Info palette.

To set the display for the Info palette:

1 Choose Options from the Info palette pop-up menu. The Info Options dialog box appears.

Using the options in this dialog box, you can display the values for pixels in two different color modes. This can be especially useful when you're working in an RGB image but want to see the CMYK values for the pixels at the same time.

2 Choose RGB Color from the First Color Readout Mode menu and be sure that Show First Color Readout is selected.

In actuality, you have been seeing the RGB colors in the top of the Info palette, even though the First Color Readout Mode menu probably reads Actual Color. See the *Adobe Photoshop User Guide* for an explanation of the Actual Color option.

3 Choose CMYK Color from the Second Color Readout Mode menu and be sure that Show Second Color Readout is selected.

TIP: YOU CAN ALSO DISPLAY THE INFO PALETTE OPTIONS FOR MODES BY CLICKING THE EYEDROPPER ICON IN THE INFO PALETTE. TO DISPLAY THE MOUSE COORDINATE OPTIONS, CLICK THE CROSSHAIR IN THE INFO PALETTE.

This dialog box also lets you turn on and off the mouse coordinates displayed in the Info palette, as well as change the measurement units for the mouse coordinates. You don't need to worry about these settings right now.

4 Click OK to close the dialog box.

To compare color values in the Info palette:

1 Click the eyedropper tool and position the eyedropper over the chef's left cheek in the CHEF.PSD window.

The Info palette shows RGB values of approximately 255 for R, 207 for G, and 177 for B. The CMYK values show the percentage of black in the pixel, about 0 percent for C, 23 percent for M, 29 percent for Y, and 0 percent for K. Unless you have the eyedropper in the exact same location, your values may be slightly different. Since this measurement is only for comparison, the actual values you see in the Info palette don't matter for this example.

2 Activate the CCHEF.PSD window and move the eyedropper to the same location in this image.

Now the values show the color correction. The R value is approximately 231, the G value is 182, and the B value is 163. The CMYK values are about 8 percent for C, 33 percent for M, 30 percent for Y, and 1 percent for K. You can see that the final color-corrected image will have less red, more green, and less blue. In CMYK values, the image will have more cyan, more magenta, about the same amount of yellow, and a small amount of black.

3 Activate the CHEF.PSD window and click the eyedropper on the top yellow pepper at the right side of the bowl.

This sets the color as the foreground color so you can use it as a visual color reference.

4 Move into the CCHEF.PSD window, hold down the Alt key, and click the same location to set the background color (you'll need to drag the window to the left temporarily to show the pepper).

Comparing the color swatches in the foreground and background selection boxes is a quick way to see how a specific color differs in the two images.

ADJUSTING THE COLOR BALANCE IN AN IMAGE

With the highlights, shadows, and midtones corrected, you're now ready to adjust the color balance in this image. For the corrected image, you want to produce balanced skin tones and neutral, or slightly cool, whites and grays in the clothing.

To adjust the color balance:

1 Zoom in on both images so that you're in the 2:1 view.

Zoom in on the CCHEF.PSD first, then zoom in on the CHEF.PSD so that the images overlap and you can see both faces.

2 Drag the Info palette to the lower-right corner of the screen.

3 Make sure the CHEF.PSD window is active, then choose Adjust from the Image menu and Color Balance from the submenu (or press Control+Y). The Color Balance dialog box appears.

The Color Balance command allows you to change the mixture of color in an image so you can delete unwanted colors or enhance dull or muted colors.

4 Make sure the Preview option is selected, and drag the dialog box down so you can see the adjustments as you make them.

5 Select the Midtones option at the bottom of the dialog box.

You can also use this command to change the color balance of the shadows or highlights.

6 To add magenta and remove green, drag the Magenta/Green slider to the left until the middle text box reads –28 (or until the color looks right on your screen).

7 To add blue and remove yellow, drag the Yellow/Blue slider to the right until the right text box reads +13.

8 To add cyan and remove red, drag the Cyan/Red slider to the left until the left text box reads –12.

9 Do not click OK to apply these settings yet.

COMPARING BEFORE-AND-AFTER COLOR VALUES USING THE EYEDROPPER

Whenever you have a color-correction dialog box open, the Info palette shows you two sets of color values. The values on the left show the original pixel values; the values on the right show the values after correction. To see how this works, you're going to roam around a bit in this image and watch the Info palette values.

Remember, since you are correcting the midtones, the differences will show up only in areas with middle tones.

1 Move the eyedropper over the line of blush on the chef's right cheek.

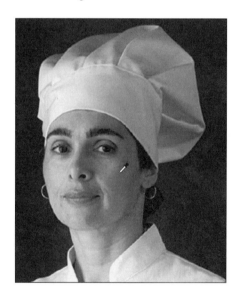

The Info palette should look something like this.

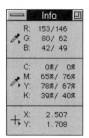

Again, your values may be different, depending on the exact location of the eyedropper.

Since the values on the left show the original pixels, and the values on the right show the corrected pixels, you can preview the severity of the adjustment. For example, in the Color Balance dialog box you added magenta and removed green. The values in the Info palette show that you are going from an M value of about 74 to 82, and a G value of about 82 to 64. (Your values may differ, depending on the adjustments you made in the Color Balance dialog box.)

2 Move the eyedropper over the shadows in the lower right of the chef's hat.

The Info palette shows the increase in cyan and magenta values and the decrease in yellow values.

3 Press the spacebar to display the hand pointer, and scroll around in the image to see how other areas are affected by these color changes.

As you scroll, look for the changes in the midtones.

4 Click OK in the Color Balance dialog box to apply the color corrections.

5 Save the file as CHEF1.PSD.

ADJUSTING THE COLOR BALANCE IN A SELECTION

As with all Adobe Photoshop editing techniques, you can apply color-correction commands to all or part of an image. The Color Balance and Hue/-Saturation commands provide two good ways to color-correct only part of an image. For this image, you're going to increase the variety of the peppers in the bowl by changing two yellow peppers into orange peppers.

To color-correct a selection:

1 Return both images to a 1:1 view, and make sure the CHEF1.PSD window is active.

2 Double-click the lasso tool to display the Lasso Options dialog box.

3 Enter a value of 2 for the Feather Radius.

4 Use the lasso to trace around the two yellow peppers on the right side of the bowl.

You can zoom in if you want to. This selection doesn't have to be precise, but try to include some of the shadow between the yellow and green peppers.

5 Open the Magic Wand Options dialog box and set the tolerance to 32.

6 Hold down the Control key and use the magic wand to remove the dark centers of the peppers from the selection.

You want to change the color of the peppers, but not of the pepper stems. The peppers are currently a bright, almost neon yellow. To make the color warmer, you're going to decrease the cyan and increase the red for this selection.

7 Hide the edges of the selection so you can see the correction preview more easily.

8 Press Control+Y to display the Color Balance dialog box.

9 Drag the top Cyan/Red slider to the right until the text box reads +18, then click OK to change the color.

This improves the color of the peppers but is not the final effect you're looking for. The color is not quite realistic.

ADJUSTING THE HUE AND SATURATION IN A SELECTION

In Lesson 5, you used the Hue/Saturation command and the Colorize option for this command to adjust the color of a textured background of an image. Now you're going to adjust the hue and saturation for this selection.

As you might remember, the sliders in the Hue/Saturation dialog box reflect the number of degrees of rotation around the color wheel that the new color is from the original color (or from the red hue of 0 degrees if you're using the Colorize option).

1 Press Control+U to display the Hue/Saturation dialog box.

2 Click the eyedropper on the selection to select a new foreground color.

Notice that the Sample box at the bottom of the dialog box shows the foreground color. Watch this box to see how the changes you make affect this specific color. To gauge how the other colors change, watch the color swatches along the left side of the dialog box. These swatches are the additive and subtractive primary colors in the order in which they appear in the color wheel. You can select individual colors to adjust. For now, leave the Master option selected, which adjusts all the colors at the same time.

3 Drag the Hue slider to the left until the text box reads −14.

This makes the peppers a bright orange color—a little too bright to be believable.

4 Drag the Saturation slider to the left until the text box reads −10 to reduce the intensity of the color.

5 Click OK to apply the color correction, then deselect the peppers.

6 Save this file as CHEF2.PSD.

LIGHTENING AND DARKENING AREAS IN AN IMAGE

While the color correction in this image now has a good balance, there are a few areas that need minor corrections. You are going to add some snap to the image by lightening the shadow areas in the peppers, and darkening the shadow tones in the chef's smock. To do this, you'll use the dodge/burn tool.

Dodging and burning-in are familiar techniques to photographers, who use these methods to correct unbalanced areas in a print caused by overexposing or underexposing the negative.

 In Adobe Photoshop you use the *dodge tool* to lighten areas of an image.

 You use the *burn tool* to darken areas of an image.

To dodge the shadows in the peppers:

1 Zoom in on the peppers in the CHEF2.PSD and CCHEF.PSD windows.

Since the changes you're making with this tool are minor, you might want to use the reference file as a guide.

2 Make sure the CHEF2.PSD window is active, then click the dodge tool in the tool palette and move into the image area. Notice that the pointer turns into a black circle on a stick.

This icon represents a piece of cardboard taped to a handle that photographers traditionally use as a dodge tool.

3 Select the second brush from the left in the second row of the Brushes palette, and make sure that the Exposure is at 50 percent and Midtone is selected in the Mode menu.

Increasing the exposure produces a stronger effect; decreasing it produces a more subtle lightening.

4 Using short strokes, paint with the dodge tool to lighten the shadow areas in the peppers.

The effect is particularly noticeable in the shadows of the red and green peppers.

To burn in the shadows on the chef's smock:

1 Zoom out so you can see the entire image in both windows.

2 Double-click the dodge tool. The Dodge/Burn Options dialog box appears.

3 Choose Burn from the Tool pop-up menu and click OK.

4 Double-click the brush on the far right in the second row of the Brushes palette to change the brush options.

5 Set the Diameter to 40, the Hardness to 0, and the Spacing to 25 percent, then click OK.

6 Move into the image area and notice that the pointer turns into a hand with the thumb and index finger touching.

This icon reflects the fact that most photographers use their fingers and hands as burn-in tools.

7 Stroke the burn tool over the shadows in the smock under the peppers.

If you want to experiment, try using a smaller brush and stroking the right sleeve and collar of the smock. Stroking in white areas won't add shadows. The burn tool builds on the existing pixel values; the white areas don't have any original dark areas to build on.

8 Save the image as CHEF3.PSD.

BLURRING AND SHARPENING AREAS IN AN IMAGE

Sometimes, areas in an image may be slightly out of focus, or you may have edges that are too sharp (that is, there is a noticeable transition that gives the image that "computer art" look). The blur/sharpen tool lets you correct these minor flaws.

Applying the *blur tool* decreases the contrast between pixels and produces a smoother image. You'll use the blur tool to soften the jagged edges on the peppers.

Applying the *sharpen tool* increases the contrast between pixels and produces more clarity or focus. You'll use the sharpen tool to bring the pepper stems into focus.

To blur the edges of the peppers:

1 Zoom in on the peppers so that both windows are in the 2:1 view.

Notice the jagged edges around the peppers.

2 Make sure the CHEF3.PSD window is active, then click the blur tool in the toolbox and move into the image area. Notice that the pointer turns into a water drop.

3 Select the third brush from the right in the top row of the Brushes palette and make sure that the Pressure is set at 50 percent and the Mode is set to Normal.

Increasing the pressure produces a stronger blurring effect; decreasing the pressure creates a weaker effect.

4 Paint along the edges of the peppers to smooth out the edges.

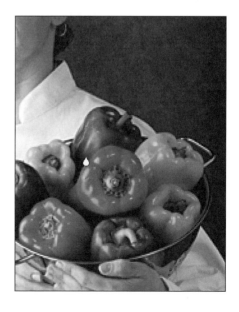

You can see the blurring most clearly along the edges of the peppers that are outlined by the white smock.

To focus the pepper stems:

1 With the blur tool still selected, hold down the Alt key. Notice that the pointer turns into a triangle.

Make sure that the Caps Lock key is not depressed. Holding down the Alt key lets you switch between the blur and sharpen tools (you can also hold down the Alt key to switch between the dodge and burn tools). When you use this shortcut (instead of choosing the tool from the Options menu in the dialog boxes), you must use the same brush and exposure or pressure setting for both tools.

2 Paint the pepper stems to bring them into focus.

3 Save this file as CHEF4.PSD.

4 Return both images to the 1:1 view.

SHARPENING AN ENTIRE IMAGE

Sometimes, a poor-quality original photograph or the scanning process can cause an image to appear slightly out of focus or *soft*. You can sharpen an image using the Adobe Photoshop sharpening filters.

To sharpen this image:

1 Make sure that CHEF4.PSD is active and choose Sharpen from the Filter menu and Unsharp Mask from the submenu. The Unsharp Mask dialog box appears.

The Unsharp Mask filter finds areas in the image where abrupt color changes occur and sharpens them by increasing the contrast between the light and dark pixels.

2 If necessary, set the Amount to 50 percent, the Radius to 1, and the Threshold to 0, then click OK to apply the filter.

The effect of this mask is subtle, and you may not immediately see the difference in the image.

3 Press Control+F to apply the filter a few more times, until the image is "too" sharp.

4 Press Control+Z to undo the last filter application.

When sharpening an image it's often helpful to overdo the sharpening, and then go back one step to get the correct image. You have now finished your color corrections, and your file should be very close to the colors in the CCHEF.PSD file.

5 Save the file as CHEF5.PSD.

DISPLAYING THE FILE IN CMYK MODE

This is the point in the color-correction strategy where you would convert this file to CMYK mode, as a step toward printing the final image. You'll learn about this conversion process in Lesson 11. For now, you're going to open an already converted CMYK version of this file to make one final color correction.

To open the CMYK file:

1 Close the CHEF5.PSD file and open the CHEFCMYK.PSD file.

While you still have the RGB version of the CCHEF.PSD file open, compare the two images. You won't see any difference because your monitor can only display images in RGB color. If you printed the two versions of the file, the differences would be quite apparent.

2 Close the CCHEF.PSD file and open the CCHEFCMY.PSD file as your reference file.

3 Move the images side by side.

COLOR-CORRECTING AN INDIVIDUAL CHANNEL

When you made color corrections to this image earlier in this lesson, you applied the color corrections to red, green, and blue channels simultaneously. You can also make color corrections to an individual channel. A channel, you will remember, contains specific color information about the image.

Displaying the histogram for individual channels

Before you make the color correction, you're going to look at the distribution of pixels in each of the color channels.

To display the histogram for individual channels:

1 Open the Channels palette.

A CMYK image contains a composite channel and four individual channels, one for each of the process colors.

2 Choose Histogram from the Image menu to display the Histogram dialog box.

The pop-up menu at the top of the Histogram dialog box shows that the Gray channel is currently chosen. The Gray channel shows the combined histogram values for all the channels.

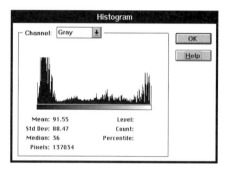

3 Choose Cyan from the pop-up menu to display the pixel values for this channel.

The gradation bar below the histogram appears in cyan to indicate the channel you're looking at. Notice that the cyan channel has a high concentration of pixels in the shadows.

4 Choose Magenta from the pop-up menu.

The histogram shifts and shows that the greatest concentration of pixels in this channel is in the middle or flesh tones.

5 Choose Yellow from the pop-up menu.

The histogram shifts again to show the yellow pixel values. For both the magenta and yellow channels, the pixels start further from the right edge of the histogram than they do in the cyan channel. This placement accounts for the blue cast in the bright white fabric of the chef's clothing.

6 Choose Black from the pop-up menu to check this channel's distribution.

7 Click OK to close the Histogram dialog box.

Adjusting colors in the channels

Now you're ready to adjust the cyan channel to remove the blue cast from the image. You'll use the Levels command to make this correction.

To color-correct a channel:

1 Drag the Info palette so you will be able to see it with an open dialog box, then press Control+L to display the Levels dialog box.

2 Drag the dialog box so you can see the image.

Notice that the Levels dialog box appears with the cyan channel already chosen. If this is not the case, you may have been in the composite view when you opened the Levels dialog box. If you are seeing the composite channel, choose Cyan from the pop-up menu at the top of the dialog box.

3 Move the eyedropper over the image and look at the values in the Info palette.

When you're editing a single channel, only a black (K) value appears in the CMYK readout in the Info palette. This value tells you the percentage of this color in the image.

4 Drag the white triangle for the Input Levels to the left, until the text box reads 185, to remove some cyan from the highlight area.

The image changes to show the reduction in cyan pixels. This is too much of a correction.

5 For a final adjustment, again drag the white triangle for the Input levels to the right, until the text box reads 240.

6 Click OK to apply this correction, then return to the composite view of the image.

7 Save the file as CCMYK1.PSD.

8 Close the files.

And here's your final color-corrected image! Considering what you started with, you're probably amazed at the change in the image. You've covered a lot of territory in this lesson, and you should be proud of everything you've learned. With this knowledge, you are ready to tackle almost any color-correction challenge that you might encounter as you use Adobe Photoshop for your own work.

LE MONDE

B

Gourmet Visions

Lesson

8

SCANNING, RESOLUTION AND RESIZING

LESSON 8: SCANNING, RESOLUTION, AND RESIZING

T his lesson discusses choosing a scanning resolution and explains the relationship between resolution and resizing an image. When you first begin working with digitized images, the term *resolution* can be confusing. At various times, resolution is used to describe the amount of pixel information in an image, the number of bits of stored information in a single pixel, the output quality of a printer, or even the density of a halftone screen.

In this lesson, you'll be exploring resolution as it refers to the amount of stored information in a particular image. This type of resolution affects an image's file size, its size on the screen, and the final printed output. It should take you about an hour to complete this lesson.

In this lesson, you'll learn how to do the following:

- estimate the best scan resolution

- determine how file size affects image resolution

- resize an image with and without resampling

- crop an image proportionately

- combine images of different resolutions

At the end of this lesson, you'll have a composite portrait of the chef that takes her from a boring everyday work environment and puts her in a dramatic stage setting.

Source file (PCHEF.PSD)

Source file (VELVET.PSD) *Ending image (VCHEF.PSD)*

ABOUT RESOLUTION

Several types of resolution are important when discussing the properties of digitized images: bit resolution, device resolution, screen resolution (or screen frequency), and image resolution.

Bit resolution, or bit depth, measures the number of bits of stored information per pixel. This resolution determines how many colors can be displayed at one time on-screen (that is, 8-bit, 24-bit, or 32-bit color).

Device resolution, or output resolution, refers to the number of dots per inch (dpi) that the output device—such as a monitor, an imagesetter, or a laser printer—can produce. This resolution is measured in dpi. The device resolution for a PC monitor can vary from 60 to 120 dpi. It cannot be changed through the Adobe Photoshop software.

Screen resolution, also known as *screen frequency*, refers to the number of dots per inch in the half-tone screen used to print a grayscale image or color separation. Screen resolution is measured in lines per inch (lpi).

Image resolution refers to the amount of information stored for an image, typically measured in pixels per inch (ppi). The image resolution and the document's dimensions determine the overall file size of the document, as well as the quality of the output. The higher the image resolution, the more space on disk the image requires, and the more time it takes for printing and other operations.

SCANNING BASICS

The choices you make before scanning an image affect the quality and usefulness of the resulting digital file. Before scanning, be sure you do the following:

- define the area you want to scan

- decide what scan resolution you should use

- determine the optimal dynamic range (if your scanner lets you set black points and white points)

- check for color casts that you might want to eliminate during the scan

The following section discusses how to set the scan resolution. See the *Adobe Photoshop User Guide* for information about determining the optimal dynamic range and eliminating unwanted color casts.

Determining the correct scan resolution

The optimal scan resolution depends on how the image will be printed or displayed. If you're going to use the image as a screen display, its resolution need not be greater than the resolution of the target screen area—about 640 pixels by 480 pixels. The images in this lesson were scanned at low resolutions because they were meant to be displayed on-screen.

In many cases, however, you will be scanning images for later output on high-resolution devices. If you are producing a full-bleed magazine cover, for example, you will need considerably more data to work with—that is, the image will need to be scanned at a higher resolution.

If the image resolution is too low, Adobe Photoshop may use the color value of a single pixel to create several halftone dots. This results in *pixelization*, or very coarse-looking output. If the resolution is too high, the file contains more information than the printer needs. Image resolution that exceeds twice the screen frequency used to print the image can rob the image of subtle transitions in tone. This can result in a posterized or very flat image. When setting the scan resolution, your goal is to balance ideal resolution with a manageable file size.

Calculating the scan resolution

You calculate the correct scan resolution by using the screen frequency that will be used to print the final output, and the original and final image dimensions.

If you plan to separate a color image, a good rule of thumb is to capture pixels at twice the screen frequency to be used for printing. For example, if you are producing a magazine cover that will be printed using a 133-lpi screen, a good scanning resolution would be 266 ppi, or twice the screen frequency.

If the final image will be larger than the scanned original, you need additional data to produce a final image with the correct image resolution. If the final image will be smaller than the original, you need less data.

To calculate the scan resolution:

1 Multiply the longest dimension of the final image size by the screen frequency; then multiply this value by the ratio of screen ruling (typically 2:1).

For example, suppose you are scanning an image that is 2 inches wide by 3 inches high, and you want to produce a final image that is 4 inches wide by 5 inches high. You are using a screen frequency of 150.

2 Multiply 5 (the longest output dimension) by 150 (the screen frequency) to get 750 pixels. Then multiply 750 by 2 (the ratio of the screen ruling). This equals a total of 1500 pixels needed.

3 Divide the total number of pixels needed by the longest dimension of the original image.

In this example, the longest dimension of the original image is 3 inches. Dividing 1500 by 3 equals a scan resolution of 500 dpi.

Different color-separation procedures might require different pixel-to-line screen ratios. It's a good idea to check with your service bureau or print shop to finalize the resolution requirement before you scan the image.

BEGINNING THIS LESSON

In this lesson, you'll resize an image and change its resolution. Then you'll combine two images with different resolutions.

To begin this lesson:

1 Open the PCHEF.PSD file in the LESSON8 directory. If the image doesn't appear at 1:1 view, double-click the zoom tool.

2 Close or collapse all of the Adobe Photoshop palettes. You'll need only the toolbox for this lesson.

HOW RESOLUTION AFFECTS FILE SIZE AND DISPLAY

To work efficiently with scanned images, you determine the amount of image information you need, and then discard the rest. Doing this allows you to minimize the file size so that the image processes more quickly.

Image resolution affects file size in a proportional way. The size of a file is proportional to the square of its resolution. If you maintain the dimensions of an image but double its file size, the image resolution increases four times. For example, if you increase the resolution of a 72-ppi image to 144 ppi while keeping the same dimensions, the file size increases by four times.

Image resolution also affects how large the image appears on the screen. Since the resolution of your screen is always 72 dpi, a 144-ppi image is displayed at double its actual size. These relationships will become clearer as you work through this lesson.

CHANGING IMAGE SIZE AND RESOLUTION

Changing an image's resolution (or *resampling*) changes the amount of information contained in the image.

In general, it's not a good idea to decrease an image's resolution and later increase the resolution. For example, suppose you decreased an image's resolution because you were printing on a low-resolution device such as a 300-dpi laser printer. Decreasing the resolution deletes some of the original color information in the image. If you later increase the resolution, Adobe Photoshop calculates the color value of the missing pixels to add information. The resulting image is not as sharp as the original, higher-resolution image.

The Image Size command lets you resize an image while controlling the image resolution. You were introduced to this command in Lesson 5, when you used it to resize the brochure art. In this lesson, you'll use the Image Size command to change the size and resolution of the PCHEF.PSD image. Before you begin making changes, however, you need to find out the current file size and dimensions of the image.

To change the image size and resolution:

1 Note the file size in the lower-left corner of the window, then hold down the Alt key and press the mouse button to display the size preview box.

The file size is 841K, and the image is about 7 inches wide and about 7.9-inches high. The image resolution is 72 ppi.

2 Choose Image Size from the Image menu.

3 In the Image Size dialog box, choose inches from the pop-up menus.

4 Make sure that the Constrain Proportions option is selected.

This option changes the image dimensions without changing the height-to-width ratio. When you enter a new value for the height or width, the program automatically adjusts the other value to maintain the image proportions.

Resampling an image as you resize

When you *resample down* (decrease the resolution or decrease the dimensions and keep the same resolution), the program deletes information from the image. When you *resample up* (increase the resolution or increase the dimensions and keep the same resolution), Adobe Photoshop creates new pixel information based on the existing color values.

To resample the image:

1 Deselect the Constrain File Size option.

When you deselect this option, Adobe Photoshop either adds or deletes information from the file.

2 Enter 90 in the Resolution text box.

Increasing the resolution of this image (while keeping the same dimensions) increases the file size to 1.28 M (the M stands for megabytes) as shown at the top of the New Size box. This means Adobe Photoshop will add information to this file.

3 Click OK to resample up the image.

Because you increased the resolution beyond the monitor resolution of between 60 and 120 dpi, the image appears larger on the screen. The actual size of the image (7inches by 7.9 inches) has not changed.

4 Choose Undo Image Size to return to the original image.

5 Choose Image Size again and enter 3 in the Width box. The height changes to 3.387 inches. Leave the resolution at 72 ppi.

Decreasing the dimensions of the image (while keeping the same resolution) decreases the file size to 155K, indicating that the program will delete information from the file.

6 Click OK to resample down the image.

The smaller image reflects the new dimensions you have set while keeping the 72-ppi resolution.

7 Choose Undo again to return to the original image.

Resizing without resampling

If you constrain a file size while you resize, Adobe Photoshop does not resample the image. The program automatically adjusts the other parameter so that no information is added to or deleted from the file.

To resize without resampling:

1 Choose Image Size again and select the Constrain File Size option.

2 Enter 3 in the Width text box; again, the height changes to 3.387 inches to keep the same image proportions.

Decreasing the dimensions while constraining the file size increases the resolution to 168 ppi, but the current file size and new file size remain the same.

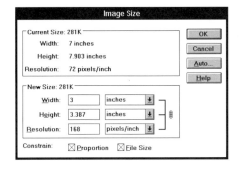

When you decrease the image dimensions without changing the file size, the same number of pixels must fill a smaller area so the resolution increases. (In the same way, if you increase the dimensions while constraining the file size, the resolution decreases because the same number of pixels must fill a larger area.)

3 Click OK.

The display of the image does not change even though you have reduced the image dimensions because the file still contains the same number of pixels.

4 Display the size preview box to confirm the new dimensions and resolution.

5 Save the image as PCHEF1.PSD in the Projects directory.

Changing resolution as you crop an image

The cropping tool contains options that let you define the height-to-width ratio for the cropping marquee and the resolution of the cropped image. These options allow you to *crop proportionately.*

To specify the size of a cropped area:

1 Double-click the cropping tool in the toolbox. The Cropping Tool Options dialog box appears.

2 Enter 2 inches for the Width and 2.5 inches for the Height. Leave the Resolution text box blank, then click OK.

When you specify a size but not a resolution, Adobe Photoshop determines the maximum resolution possible for the defined marquee size.

3 Zoom out so you can see the entire image.

4 Position the pointer on the yellow pasta, then drag up and to the right to include the pasta machine and all of the pasta chef in the marquee.

The marquee is constrained proportionately by the dimensions you specified in the Cropping Tool Options dialog box. If the cropping border doesn't include all of the chef and the pasta machine, reposition the border by holding down the Control key as you drag a handle.

5 Click the scissors inside the marquee to crop the image.

6 Preview the new image size.

The new file size is about 600K, and the new dimensions are 2 inches by 2.5 inches (the marquee size you specified). The new resolution is about 200 ppi (depending on the exact size of the marquee you drew). This is the maximum resolution possible, given the selected area. The resolution increased because you reduced the image size.

7 Use the marquee to crop the image again, this time including just the pasta machine and part of the chef's hands.

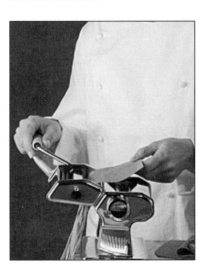

8 Click with the scissors inside the marquee to crop the image.

9 Alt+click in the size preview box to preview the image size.

The new file size is about 150K. The dimensions are still 2 inches by 2.5 inches, but this time the resolution has decreased to about 100 ppi.

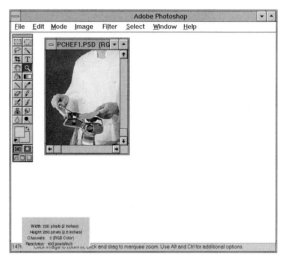

The resolution has decreased because this is the maximum resolution possible, given the selected area and the amount of information the image needs to contain. Since the area you just cropped is an enlargement of the original image, the resolution decreased.

10 Choose Revert from the File menu to return to the original PCHEF1.PSD image.

Using Auto Resolution

Now you're ready to put the chef against her new background. Your first step is to return the PCHEF1.PSD image to its original resolution of 72 ppi. One way to do this is to have Adobe Photoshop determine the resolution by using the Auto button in the Image Size dialog box.

To determine a suggested resolution for an image:

1 Choose Image Size from the Image menu, then click the Auto button in the Image Size dialog box. The Auto Resolution dialog box appears.

2 Use the default Screen value of 133 lpi.

This screen value is used only to calculate the image resolution. (To specify the halftone screen frequency for printing, you must use the Halftone Screens dialog box. You'll learn more about this dialog box in Lesson 11.)

3 Click Draft for the Quality setting.

Draft produces a resolution that is one times the screen frequency (no higher than 72 pixels per inch). Because you will work with the image only on-screen, you do not need a resolution higher than 72 ppi.

4 Click OK to return to the Image Size dialog box.

The recommended resolution of 72 ppi is entered automatically in the Image Size dialog box, and the file size decreases to 155K.

5 Click OK to resize the image.

The image appears smaller on your screen since you have reduced the resolution.

6 Save the image as PCHEF2.PSD.

COMBINING IMAGES WITH DIFFERENT RESOLUTIONS

When you combine two images, the results may be unexpected if the resolution of the images does not match. The background you are going to paste this image into has a different resolution from this file.

To compare the resolution of the files:

1 Open the VELVET.PSD file in the LESSON8 directory.

2 Drag the image by its title bar so that it appears next to the PCHEF2.PSD image. The VELVET.PSD file appears much larger than the PCHEF2.PSD image.

3 Preview the size for both images.

The VELVET.PSD image is 3 inches by 3.7 inches—essentially the same size as the PCHEF2.-PSD image—but the resolution is 144 ppi, or double that of the PCHEF2.PSD image. You will see how the different resolutions affect the combination of the two images when you paste the chef into the VELVET.PSD image.

4 In the Magic Wand Options dialog box, enter a Tolerance of 50 and make sure the Anti-aliased option is on, then click OK.

5 Activate the PCHEF2.PSD window and click the magic wand in the gray background.

The entire background is selected.

6 Inverse the selection so that the chef and the table are selected.

7 Copy the selection to the Clipboard, then paste it into the VELVET.PSD image.

The *selection* appears much too small for the velvet background. Pasting the PCHEF2.PSD selection into the VELVET.PSD image caused the 72-ppi resolution of the selection to double to 144 ppi, to match the resolution of the VELVET.PSD image. Although the dimensions of the two original images almost match, the proportions appear distorted because the resolutions are different.

Reducing the resolution of a file

To make a composite of the two images, you need to reduce the resolution of the VELVET.PSD image to match that of the PCHEF2.PSD image.

1 Undo the paste action.

2 With the Velvet window active, choose Image Size from the Image menu and make sure the Constrain File Size option is not selected.

3 Enter 72 in the Resolution text box.

The new file size is about 173K to reflect the decreased resolution.

4 Click OK.

The VELVET.PSD image is resampled down to 72 ppi. The side-by-side images now appear to be about the same size. (If the sizes are not similar, make sure you're viewing both images at 1:1 view.)

5 Paste the selection into the VELVET.PSD file again.

The two images now appear correctly proportioned.

6 Drag the selection down if necessary, to make the table flush with the bottom of the window, then deselect the selection.

7 Save this file as VELVETC1.PSD in the Projects directory.

CHANGING THE SIZE OF THE CANVAS

To complete the lesson, you're going to put a border around the composite image. In Lesson 5, you learned how to create a border using the Stroke command. In this lesson, you'll use the Canvas Size command to create the border.

To use the Canvas Size command:

1 Set the background color to black (all added canvas appears in the background color).

2 Choose Canvas Size from the Image menu.

3 Enter 3.25 inches in the Width text box and 4.08 inches in the Height text box, then click the center square in the placement box.

This adds a border of one-eighth of an inch around the image.

4 Click OK to add the black canvas to the image.

5 Save the final image.

6 Close the files.

This lesson deals with several concepts that are central to working with digitized images, yet can sometimes be quite confusing. Understanding the relationship between image size and resolution, image display and resolution, resampling up, and resampling down can take some time. If you feel you need more review, try doing some of the tasks in this lesson again, or better yet, use the steps to experiment with your own favorite images.

LE MONDE

B

Gourmet Visions

Lesson 9: Review Project— Annual Report Cover

I n this lesson, you will have a chance to practice the techniques you learned in Lessons 7 and 8. Nothing new is introduced in this lesson.

The step-by-step instructions in this lesson provide all the information you need to complete the project. Because this is a review, detailed instructions aren't included. If you find that you can't remember how to do something, or need more precise instructions, refer back to Lessons 7 and 8. It should take you about 45 minutes to complete this lesson.

In Lesson 7, most of your efforts were directed toward *color-correcting* the *Portrait* image. In Lesson 8, you learned about resizing and cropping an image. In this lesson, you'll use many of the same techniques to combine three images to create the annual report cover for a Gourmet Visions subsidiary called Casalingo Incorporated. You'll work with one familiar image and two new images in this lesson.

Source file (PEPPERS.PSD)

Ending image (AREPORT.PSD)

Source file
(PFACTORY.PSD)

Source file
(OLIVEOIL.PSD)

BEGINNING THIS LESSON

In this lesson, you'll modify your beginning image by adding cropped sections from two other images, and then add text to create the final composite image. All the files you'll work with in this lesson are in RGB mode.

To begin this lesson:

1 Open the AREPORT.PSD file in the LESSON9 directory, zoom out to reduce the image, click the resize box to reduce the window, then drag the window to the upper-right corner of your screen.

2 Open the PFACTORY.PSD image in the LES-SON9 directory. If the image does not appear at 1:1 view, double-click the zoom tool.

3 Turn on the rulers in the PFACTORY.PSD window.

4 Make sure that the Info and Brushes palettes are open or collapsed on your screen.

RESIZING A BACKGROUND

You'll begin making the composite image by resizing the PFACTORY.PSD image so it can serve as the background for the annual report cover. After resizing the image, you'll remove some of the extra space at the bottom.

To resize the image:

1 In the Image Size dialog box, deselect the Constrain File Size option. The Constrain Proportions option should be selected.

You need to turn off the File Size option so you can resample as you resize. The current image is 4.25 inches wide by 6.34 inches high, with a resolution of 100 ppi. The file size is 790K.

2 Enter 4.5 inches for the Width (the Height automatically changes to 6.713 inches) and enter a Resolution of 72 ppi.

Note that the new file size will be 459K. The file gets smaller because, even though you're making the dimensions larger, you're decreasing the image resolution.

3 Click OK to resize the image.

To crop the bottom of the image:

1 In the Canvas Size dialog box, leave the width at 4.5, enter 5.75 inches for the Height, and click the top-middle square in the placement box.

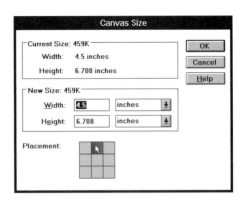

2 Click OK, then click Proceed at the warning.

The bottom part of the image is cropped. The remaining image has the correct proportions and resolution for the annual report cover.

3 Save the image as PFACT1.PSD in the Projects directory.

COLOR-CORRECTING AN IMAGE

In this part of the lesson, you will precisely correct the color in the PFACT1.PSD image by using the Levels dialog box.

Adjusting the overall contrast

As you learned in Lesson 7, when making color corrections, it's a good idea to correct overall contrast by first by setting the black and white points, and then adjusting the midtones.

To adjust the overall contrast:

1 Choose Adjust from the Image menu and Levels from the submenu.

The histogram in the Levels dialog box shows the overall darkness of the image.

2 Click the black point eyedropper, then position the eyedropper on the left side of the hair.

3 Move the eyedropper around the shadow area and watch the K values in the Info palette. Click the darkest point to set the black point (the values should be about 95 percent).

4 Hold down the Control and spacebar keys and click to zoom in on the baker's head.

5 Click the white point eyedropper in the Levels dialog box and position the eyedropper on the very top brim of the hat.

6 Move the eyedropper until the C, M, and Y values in the Info palette read about 1 percent or 2 percent, then click to set the white point.

7 Set the gamma value to 1.40 by dragging the gamma slider to the left or entering the value in the gamma text box.

8 Click OK to apply the color corrections to the image.

9 Save the file.

RETOUCHING SHADOWS IN AN IMAGE

The scanning mounts that held the PFACTO-RY.PSD negative in place during scanning created some shadows in the corners of the image. You will remove them now, using the rubber stamp tool.

To retouch shadows created by the scanner:

1 Zoom in on the upper-left corner of the image so that you have a 2:1 or 4:1 view.

2 Select a small brush in the Brushes palette—for example, the third brush from the left in the second row.

3 Using the rubber stamp tool with the Clone (aligned) option, Alt+click the pasta about half an inch below and to the right of the mount shadow to set the sampling point.

TIP: BY PRESSING THE ALT KEY AND CLICKING THE MOUSE BUTTON WHEN YOU WANT TO ANCHOR THE LINE TO THE IMAGE, YOU CAN CREATE STRAIGHT RUBBER BAND LINES WITH THE LASSO TOOL.

4 Drag over the shadow to remove it.

5 Scroll to the right side of the image and repeat steps 3 and 4 to remove the shadow from the upper-right corner.

6 Zoom out to a 1:1 view, then save the image as PFACT2.PSD.

ADJUSTING SATURATION IN SELECTED AREAS

In the final cover, you want to focus attention on the tray of spaghetti. To do this, you need to decrease the saturation of color in the other areas of the image to emphasize the color in the spaghetti tray.

To adjust the saturation:

1 Set the Feather Radius to 2 in the Lasso Options dialog box and use the lasso to trace around the tray of spaghetti.

You don't have to be precise, but try not to select the area on either side of the chef's hands.

2 Inverse the selection so that everything but the tray is selected.

3 Choose Adjust from the Image menu and Hue/Saturation from the submenu.

4 In the Hue/Saturation dialog box, be sure the Preview option is selected, then drag the Saturation slider to the left to –75.

This adjustment removes color from the background areas, creating the appearance of a partially colored photograph. Only a hint of color remains in the background areas, giving them the appearance of a grayscale and emphasizing the spaghetti in the foreground.

5 Drag the Lightness slider to the right to +25 to make the selection fade further.

6 Click OK to apply the changes.

7 Deselect the selection and save this image as REPORT1.PSD.

CREATING A SILHOUETTE

To complete the background, you will create a silhouette of the image.

To create a silhouette:

1 Double-click the elliptical marquee tool and set the Feather Radius to 15 pixels.

2 Position the elliptical marquee tool on the center of the image about 2-1/4 inches from the left edge of the window and 2-7/8 inches from the top of the window.

3 Hold down the Alt key and draw an oval selection from the center of the image that extends to about a quarter inch to a half inch from the edges of the image. (The bottom of the Info palette should show a selection about 3.75 inches wide and 5 inches high.)

4 Inverse the selection.

5 Click the default colors icon to set the background color to white, then press Backspace or Delete.

The selection is deleted and replaced with the background color. The large feathering value creates a soft edge around the silhouette.

6 Deselect the selection and save the image as REPORT2.PSD.

With the background completed, you're ready to begin adding the inset images to the cover.

ADDING THE INSET IMAGES

Now you are ready to add the two inset images to the report cover. To add a little interest to these images, you're going to do some minor manipulations as you paste them into the final cover.

Adding emphasis through color and cropping

The first small image you'll add to the report is familiar to you from Lesson 7. The version of the PEPPERS.PSD file in this lesson contains a saved selection of the center red pepper. Using the technique you just learned, you're going to make this pepper stand out by decreasing the saturation in the rest of the image. Then you'll crop the image and give it a border.

To adjust the pepper:

1 Open the PEPPERS.PSD image in the LESSON9 directory.

2 Choose Load Selection from the Select menu.

This loads the Red Pepper selection stored in channel 4.

3 Inverse the selection and hide its edges.

Now everything but the pepper is selected.

4 In the Hue/Saturation dialog box, set the Saturation to −80 and click OK.

The grayscale appearance of the other peppers serves to emphasize the red of the center pepper.

5 Deselect the selection.

6 In the Cropping Tool Options dialog box, set the Width to 1.25 inches and the Height to .625 of an inch.

7 Enter a Resolution of 72 ppi to make the resolution of the PEPPERS.PSD image match the resolution of the REPORT2.PSD image, then click OK.

8 Position the cropping tool slightly above the far-left pepper and drag down and to the right, so that the red pepper is in the center of the cropping marquee.

Include a gray pepper on each side of the red pepper (the chef's hands and the bowl should not be inside the marquee). If necessary, hold down the Control key and drag one of the corner handles to reposition the marquee.

9 Click with the scissors icon to crop the image.

Adding emphasis with a border

To complete the PEPPERS.PSD crop, you need to outline the cropped image with a black border. In this instance, you'll add the border using the Stroke command as you did in Lesson 5.

To create the border and paste the inset image:

1 Set the foreground color to black.

2 Select all of the cropped PEPPERS.PSD image.

3 Choose Stroke from the Edit menu, enter a pixel width of 2, and select the Inside location option.

4 Set the Opacity of 100 percent and the mode to Normal, then click OK.

A thin border appears around the cropped image.

5 Copy the image to the Clipboard and close the PEPPERS.PSD file without saving changes.

6 Paste the selection into the REPORT2.PSD image.

7 Set the rectangular marquee to a Normal marquee and use the rectangular marquee tool to drag the selection down, until the pasted image is flush with the bottom of the window and is about a quarter inch from the left edge.

8 Deselect the selection and save the image as REPORT3.PSD.

Correcting imperfections through rotation and filtering

Again, in this section, you will make color adjustments as you add a second insert image to the report cover. In addition, you'll correct a slight angle and focus problem as you copy and paste the cropped image. Like the PEPPERS.PSD image, the OLIVEOIL.PSD image has a selection stored in channel 4.

To adjust the saturation and color balance:

1 Open the OLIVEOIL.PSD image in the LESSON9 directory.

2 Load the background selection and hide its edges.

3 In the Hue/Saturation dialog box, set the Saturation to –80 and click OK.

Now the focus of attention in this image is the bottle. The bottle still needs a few other color corrections.

4 Inverse the selection.

5 Choose Adjust from the Image menu and Color Balance from the submenu.

6 In the Color Balance dialog box, select the Midtones option and drag the Cyan/Red slider to –10 and the Magenta/Green slider to +10.

7 Click Shadows and drag the Magenta/Green slider to +10 again, then click OK.

This adjustment removes some of the red cast left from the reflection of the tomatoes in the glass. If this change isn't immediately apparent to you, use the Control+Z shortcut to Undo and Redo the color balance change.

8 Deselect the image.

Rotating while cropping

You can see that the bottle is at a slight angle. As you crop the image, you will rotate it, to compensate for the angle.

To rotate the selection as you crop:

1 In the Cropping Tool Options dialog box, set the Width to .764 of an inch and the Height to 1.5 inches.

2 Starting in about the middle of the chef's cuff, drag down and to the right to enclose the bottle and some of the garlic and bowl in the cropping marquee.

If necessary, hold down the Control key and drag a handle to center the bottle in the selection.

3 Using the angle information in the Info palette as a guide, hold down the Alt key and drag the upper-right handle in a clockwise direction, until the vertical cropping border appears parallel to the side of the bottle. The angle should be about –3.5 degrees.

4 Click with the scissors icon to crop the image.

To sharpen the image with a filter:

1 Apply the Unsharp Mask filter at 50 percent to sharpen the image slightly.

2 With the background set to black, select all of the OLIVEOIL.PSD image.

3 Stroke the image using a Width of a 2 and starting from the Inside of the selection. The Opacity should be 100 percent and the Mode should be Normal.

4 Copy the selection to the Clipboard and close the OLIVEOIL.PSD file without saving the changes.

5 Paste the cropped OLIVEOIL.PSD selection into the REPORT3.PSD image.

6 Use the rectangular marquee tool to drag the pasted floating selection up and to the right, until it is about three-eighths of an inch from the top of the window and flush with the right edge.

7 Deselect the selection and save the file as REPORT4.PSD.

CREATING SHADOWS FOR THE INSETS

Next, you will create shadows for the inset photos in the REPORT4.PSD image by using the Levels dialog box.

To create the inset shadow for the first image:

1 Create a fixed rectangular marquee with a Width of 92 pixels and a Height of 46 pixels.

2 Position the pointer about one-eighth of an inch above and one-eighth of an inch from the right edge of the PEPPERS.PSD image, then click to make a selection slightly offset from the inset image.

3 Return the rectangular marquee to the Normal setting.

4 Hold down the Control key, and starting at the upper-right corner of the PEPPERS.PSD image, drag diagonally down to the bottom-left corner of the image to subtract the image from the selection.

You are left with a one-eighth of an inch wide selection in the shape of a drop shadow, just above and to the right of the PEPPERS.PSD image.

5 Choose Adjust from the Image menu and Levels from the submenu.

6 Drag the gamma slider right to 0.55 to darken the selection, then click OK.

7 Deselect the selection.

To create the inset shadow for the second image:

1 Create a fixed rectangular marquee with a Width of 55 pixels and a Height of 101 pixels.

2 Position the pointer about one-eighth of an inch below the top of the image and one-eighth of an inch from the left edge of the OLIVEOIL.PSD image, then click to make a selection slightly offset from the inset image.

3 Return the rectangular marquee to the Normal setting.

4 Hold down the Control key, and starting at the bottom-left corner of the OLIVEOIL.PSD image, drag diagonally up to the right corner of the image to subtract the image from the selection.

You are left with a one-eighth of an inch wide selection in the shape of a drop shadow, just below and to the left of the OLIVEOIL.PSD image.

5 In the Levels dialog box, drag the gamma slider right to 0.55 to darken the selection, then click OK.

6 Deselect the selection.

7 Save the file as REPORT5.PSD.

ADDING THE TITLE TYPE

To complete the annual report cover, you will add type to the upper-left and lower-right corners.

To add the type:

1 Use the eyedropper to sample the red from the pepper to set a new foreground color.

2 In the Type Tool dialog box, set the Font to Times Bold, the Size to 10 points, and the Spacing to 1.5.

3 Enter **ANNUAL REPORT** in the text box and click OK.

4 Use the pointer to position the type three-eighths of an inch from the top of the window and one-eighth of an inch from the left edge.

5 Click the default colors icon to set the foreground color to black.

6 With the type tool still selected, click the lower right corner of the image.

7 Set the Font to Helvetica Bold Italic, the Size to 9 points, and the Spacing to 1.5.

8 Enter **CASALINGO INCORPORATED** (in all caps) and click OK.

9 Position the type so that the last letter, *D*, is one-eighth of an inch from the right edge of the window, and the bottom of the type is a quarter inch from the bottom of the window.

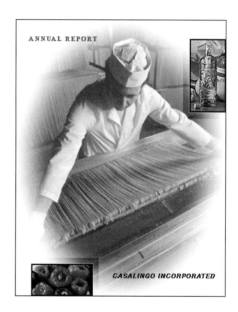

Creating transparent type

For the final element in the annual report cover, you're going to add the year in slightly transparent type.

To add transparent type:

1 Using the type tool, click the center of the image.

2 In the Type Tool dialog box, set the Font to Times Italic, the Size to 120 points, and the Spacing to 0. Enter 1994 in the text box and click OK.

3 Position the type so that the number one is over the chef's left arm (the type should be centered in the cover).

4 Drag the Opacity slider in the Brushes palette to 60 percent.

5 Deselect the selection to see the final report cover.

6 Save the file as REPORT6.PSD.

Good for you! You have completed a complex and compelling composite image suitable for the shareholders of Casalingo Incorporated. You've also had the chance to practice working with some common color-correction techniques that will help you achieve consistent and professional results with your own images.

LE MONDE

B

Gourmet Visions

LESSON 10: CONVERTING IMAGES

This lesson discusses color modes, image types, and converting images from one type of color mode to another. The lesson builds on the concept of channels, which you have been creating and using to store saved selections. The channels that Adobe Photoshop assigns to images (such as the red, green, and blue channels of an RGB image) are used as sources of color information. Using these color channels, you can make very specific adjustments to the individual color components of an image.

In this lesson, you'll use four RGB images, scanned from a photograph of an appetizer plate. After creating a different image type for each file, you'll combine the images into a composite file. This composite image will serve as the basis of a tradeshow poster, which you'll complete in Lesson 13. It should take you about an hour to complete this lesson.

In this lesson, you'll learn how to do the following:

- convert an RGB image to Lab mode, CMYK mode, indexed color mode, and grayscale mode

- convert an image to a multichannel image

- create a duotone

- invert colors

- convert a grayscale image to bitmapped mode

The following images show the photographs you'll use and the final composition.

Source file (PLATE1.PSD)   *Source file (PLATE2.PSD)*

 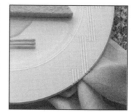

Source file (PLATE3.PSD)   *Source file (PLATE4.PSD)*

Ending image (FPLATE.PSD)

ABOUT MODES, IMAGE TYPES, AND CHANNELS

A *color mode* in Adobe Photoshop is the color model you use to display and print Adobe Photoshop documents. The most commonly used modes are Grayscale, for displaying black-and-white documents; RGB, for displaying color documents on-screen; and CMYK, for printing four-color separations. Adobe Photoshop also supports a variety of other image types, including bitmapped, duotone (including monotone, tritone, and quadtone), indexed color, and Lab color. You use the commands in the Mode menu to convert one type of image to another.

You should always save an image (with a unique name) before converting it. Since different color models comprise different colors, converting an image between modes may permanently change the color values in the image. By saving first, you'll always be able to recover your original image.

BEGINNING THIS LESSON

In this lesson, you'll convert four parts of a larger image to separate modes, and then combine the images into a final file.

To begin this lesson:

1 Open the FPLATE.PSD file in the LESSON10 directory, zoom out to reduce the image, then drag the window to the upper-right corner of your screen.

2 Open the PLATE1.PSD file and place it in the upper-left corner of your screen.

3 Make sure that the Channels and Colors palettes are open or collapsed on your screen. (You can hide or close the other Adobe Photoshop palettes.)

4 Choose Preferences from the File menu and General from the submenu. Select the Color Channels in Color option under Display.

Viewing the channels in color will help you track the changes in individual channels as you convert from one mode to another.

CONVERTING AN IMAGE FOR COLOR SEPARATIONS

Probably the most frequent mode conversion you will make will be the one required to print a color image as color separations. To print a color separation from an RGB, indexed color, or Lab image, you convert an RGB image to CMYK. (If you're printing to a PostScript Level 2 color printer, you don't have to convert a Lab image to CMYK mode because the PostScript Level 2 color printer interprets and prints Lab images.)

For the first quarter of the image, you will work with the PLATE1.PSD file and create a Lab image, a CMYK image, and an indexed color image.

CONVERTING TO LAB MODE

You can convert RGB, CMYK, and indexed color images to Lab color. You were introduced to Lab color in Lesson 7. Because the Lab *gamut*, or range of colors, encompasses both RGB and CMYK gamuts, Lab is used internally by Adobe Photoshop when it converts images between RGB and CMYK modes. Lab color is also the recommended color mode for moving images between systems (since it is device-independent), and for printing to PostScript Level 2 printers.

When you convert an RGB image to Lab mode, the image still contains three channels. Instead of red, green, and blue, however, the color information is contained in a luminance (*L*) channel, and two color channels, *a* and *b*.

To convert an RGB image to Lab mode:

1 Make the PLATE1.PSD image active. Note that the RGB file size is about 100K.

2 In the Channels palette, click the word Red.

The red color information for the PLATE1.PSD file is displayed. It's OK that the red channel for the final image appears also. When you select an individual channel in the Channels palette, all open files are displayed in that channel.

3 Click the Green and Blue channels to see their color information, then return to the RGB channel.

4 Choose Lab Color from the Mode menu.

The image is converted to Lab mode. The title bar changes to indicate the current mode of the image. The Channels palette now shows the three Lab channels for the image.

5 Click Lightness in the Channels palette.

This channel appears in grayscale since it shows the lightness or luminance values (not color values) for the image.

6 Display the *a* and *b* channels.

The *a* component shows the color range from green to magenta; the *b* component shows the color range from blue to yellow.

7 Return to the composite Lab channel.

The Lab mode is useful when you want to adjust the lightness or brightness of the image, without changing its hue or saturation (for example, to create smoother blends). Once you have adjusted the image, you can then convert it back to an RGB or a CMYK image to perform other color correc-

tions or to print the image using process colors. Converting back and forth between Lab and other image types doesn't alter the original color values.

8 Choose Revert from the File menu to return to the original RGB image.

CONVERTING TO CMYK

When you convert an RGB image to CMYK, the red, green, and blue values in the image undergo an intermediate conversion to Lab values, which are then converted to the cyan, magenta, yellow, and black values. The three-channel RGB image becomes a four-channel CMYK image.

Unlike Lab mode, converting back and forth between RGB and CMYK alters the original color values. When you plan to convert an RGB or indexed file to CMYK, be sure to save a copy of the RGB or indexed color image in case you want to reconvert the image. It's not a good idea to convert between RGB and CMYK mode multiple times, because each time the image is converted, the color values must be recalculated.

To convert an RGB image to CMYK:

1 Choose CMYK Color from the Mode menu. The file size is increased to 135K and the image contains four channels.

In the RGB to CMYK conversion process, Adobe Photoshop converts the RGB values to Lab values and builds a color table. It then uses these Lab values to determine the appropriate CMYK equivalents. Finally, the correct CMYK values for each Lab pixel are calculated by referencing the key values in the color table.

You can save individual color separation tables and use them with other Adobe Photoshop documents. You might want to save different tables if you frequently print images using different printers, different inks, or different papers. For more information, see the *Adobe Photoshop User Guide*.

2 Click Cyan in the Channels palette to display the cyan channel.

3 Display the Yellow and Black channels.

4 Display the Magenta channel.

In this channel, you can see that there is a concentration of color in the rosebud.

5 Using the elliptical marquee tool, select the rosebud and delete it.

You have now removed all of the magenta from this image in this specific location. Editing individual channels allows you to create special effects or make selective color corrections.

6 Return to the composite CMYK channel.

The remaining color information from the cyan, yellow, and black channels shows through the selection. Without the magenta component, the color appears chartreuse.

7 Click Magenta in the Channels palette again, then choose Delete Channel from the Channels pop-up menu.

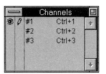

When you a delete a channel from an RGB, CMYK, Lab, or Duotone image, the image is automatically converted to Multichannel mode. The individual color channels are converted to grayscale information that reflects the color values of the pixels in each channel. In Multichannel mode, the channels from composite images (with names such as Red, Cyan, Lightness, and so on) are assigned numbers. See the *Adobe Photoshop User Guide* for more information on multichannel images.

8 Revert to the original RGB image.

CONVERTING TO INDEXED COLOR

You might want to convert an RGB image to an indexed color image to edit an image's color table, or to export an image to an application that supports only 8-bit color. Indexed color images are useful for creating a limited palette for export to multimedia applications, for example, or for animation and on-screen display.

While an RGB image contains millions of colors, an indexed color image is limited to 256 colors. This limited amount of information causes an indexed color image to appear pixelated, or coarse, when it's printed.

When converting an RGB image to an indexed color image, Adobe Photoshop builds a color table (or palette) for the indexed color image. The color table stores the colors used in the document and holds the maximum number of colors that can be displayed at once. Because an indexed color image can directly reference only 256 colors, the RGB color may not exist in the indexed color table. If the RGB color is not present, the program matches the requested color to the closest color in the color table or simulates the requested color using the available colors.

To convert an RGB image to indexed color:

1 Choose Indexed Color from the Mode menu. The Indexed Color dialog box appears.

2 Click 8 bits per pixel for the resolution.

The resolution determines the number of colors that can be displayed at one time. For example, if you select 4 bits per pixel, 16 colors can be displayed at a time; if you select 8 bits per pixel, 256 colors can be displayed at a time.

3 Click Adaptive for the palette option. By default, the Adaptive palette uses the Diffusion Dither option to generate colors.

The Adaptive palette option creates a color table by sampling colors from the more commonly used areas of the color spectrum in the image. *Dithering* mixes the pixels of the available colors to simulate the missing colors. The Diffusion dithering option randomly adds pixels to simulate the colors not in the color table. See the *Adobe Photoshop User Guide* for information about the color table and dither options.

4 Click OK to convert the image to indexed color.

The image is displayed using 256 colors. The image size is reduced to 35K, and only one channel appears in the Channel palette.

5 Choose Color Table from the Mode menu. The Color Table dialog box appears.

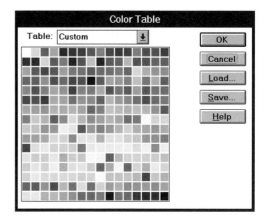

Because you chose the Adaptive palette option for the color table, the color table consists primarily of colors in the original image—browns and yellows.

6 Close the Color Table dialog box.

7 Revert to the original RGB image.

Creating special effects using Indexed Color mode

You can also use Indexed Color mode to create special effects. Working in Indexed Color mode is useful when a color image has a limited palette. For example, if you are working with an image that contains primarily yellows and greens, you might want to use an indexed color table consisting mainly of yellows and greens to give you the widest selection of tints within those hues.

You can convert an image to Indexed Color mode only from Grayscale or RGB mode. In this example, you'll convert the RGB image first to Grayscale and then to Indexed Color mode. Finally, you will create a custom color table for the image.

To convert a grayscale image to indexed color:

1 Choose Grayscale from the Mode menu. Click OK to discard the color information.

In Grayscale mode, the Channels palette shows only a single black channel.

2 Choose Indexed Color from the Mode menu to convert the image to indexed color.

The image still appears in grayscale since you have eliminated the color information. Now you're ready to add your own colors.

3 Choose Color Table from the Mode menu.

4 Choose Custom from the Table pop-up menu.

5 Starting in the upper-left corner, drag diagonally to the lower-right corner to select all the colors in the color table. The Color Picker dialog box appears.

6 Move to the CMYK text boxes in the lower-right corner and enter 100 for cyan, 86 for magenta, 0 for yellow, and 0 for black, then click OK.

This defines the first color for the color table, a dark blue.

7 To select the last color for the table, enter 90 for yellow, set cyan, magenta, and black to 0, then click OK.

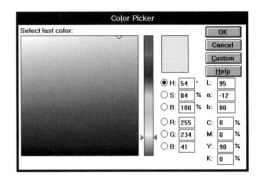

You return to the Color Table dialog box, which displays a color table ranging from blue to yellow.

8 Click OK to apply the table to the indexed color image. The result is a royal blue and yellow image.

9 Save the file as IPLATE1.PSD in the Projects directory.

You can compare this method of creating a two-color image to that of creating a duotone, which you'll do in the next section.

CREATING A DUOTONE

In this part of the lesson, you will create a duotone from the PLATE2.PSD file.

In Adobe Photoshop, the term *Duotone mode* applies generically to monotones, duotones, tritones, and quadtones. A monotone, duotone, tritone, or quadtone is a grayscale image printed with one, two, three, or four inks, respectively, to add tonal depth.

Creating a duotone involves three basic steps: you specify the type of duotone (monotone, duotone, and so on); specify the ink color to use; and adjust the duotone curve to determine how the ink is distributed across the image.

To create a duotone and load a duotone curve:

1 Open the PLATE2.PSD file in the LESSON10 directory.

2 Drag the PLATE2.PSD image to the right of the PLATE1.PSD image, so that the borders are touching.

3 Convert the PLATE2.PSD image to Grayscale mode.

To create a duotone from an RGB image, you must first convert the image to grayscale mode. Adobe Photoshop treats duotones not as true color images, but rather as grayscale images in which the gray levels are enhanced by using an ink color (typically, in addition to black). In contrast, color images use different ink colors to reproduce a variety of colors.

4 Choose Duotone from the Mode menu. The Duotone Options dialog box appears.

If you are choosing Duotone mode for the first time, Monotone appears by default in the Type pop-up menu. A duotone curve and color swatch appear in the Ink 1 field. The default duotone curve is a diagonal line extending from the lower-left corner to the upper-right corner—indicating an even distribution of ink across the range of gray in the image. The default color for Ink 1 is black.

5 Choose Duotone from the Type pop-up menu.

A duotone curve appears in the Ink 2 field. The ink color for Ink 2 is blank, since you must specify the ink color separately.

Typically, you specify the ink color and its distribution in two separate steps. You can also load a duotone curve that specifies an ink color and its distribution at the same time. The Adobe Photoshop program includes some duotone curves that you can apply to your own images.

Once you convert to Duotone, the Channels palette shows a single, duotone channel.

6 Click Load. A directory dialog box appears.

7 Select the MK-1.ADO file from the LESSON10 directory, and click OK.

The ink colors and curves appear in the Duotone Options dialog box. Notice that inks and curves for both Ink 1 and Ink 2 have been loaded. You can see that the curve for the black Ink 1 is no longer the default curve.

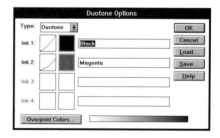

8 Click OK to apply the ink colors and distribution to the image. The image appears as a soft, almost rose tone.

9 Save the image as DPLATE2.PSD.

CREATING A TRITONE AND ADJUSTING THE INK DISTRIBUTION

In this part of the lesson, you will work with the PLATE3.PSD file and add a third ink to the duotone you just created to make the color richer. Then you'll adjust the curves that control the ink distribution. To complete the tritone, you will invert the color in the image to create the effect of a negative.

The procedures for creating a tritone and a duotone are the same.

To create a tritone:

1 Open the PLATE3.PSD image in the LESSON10 directory.

2 Drag the PLATE3.PSD image down and to the right, to place it under the PLATE2.PSD image. The borders should be touching.

3 Convert the PLATE3.PSD image to Grayscale mode.

4 Choose Duotone from the Mode menu.

5 The Duotone Options dialog box appears with the duotone curves and ink swatches you specified with the MK-1.ADO file.

6 Choose Tritone from the Type pop-up menu. A distribution curve appears in the Ink 3 field.

To specify the third ink color:

1 Click the color swatch box for Ink 3. The Custom Colors dialog box appears.

2 Make sure that PANTONE Coated is selected in the Book pop-up menu.

3 In the Find # field, enter 107. Pantone 107 CV, a bright yellow, appears selected. (You can also click a color to select it.)

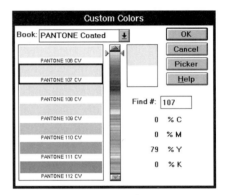

4 Click OK to add the third color to the Duotone Options dialog box.

When creating duotones, both the order in which the inks are printed and the screen angles you use dramatically affect your final output.

To produce fully saturated colors, darker inks should be printed before lighter inks. When entering colors in the duotone dialog boxes, make sure that the inks are specified in descending order—that is, the darkest ink should appear at the top and the lightest ink at the bottom. The order of inks affects how Adobe Photoshop applies screens when the duotone is printed.

To adjust the ink distribution:

1 Click the curve next to Ink 2 to display the Duotone Curve dialog box.

This duotone curve maps each grayscale value on the original image to the actual ink percentage that will be used when the image is printed. The horizontal axis shows the gray values in the original image; the vertical axis shows ink density values. The curve represents highlights in the lower-left corner, midtones in the center area, and shadows in the upper-right corner.

The default straight line curve indicates that the current grayscale value of every pixel is being mapped to the same percentage value of the printing ink. At this setting, a 50-percent midtone pixel is printed with a 50-percent dot of the ink, a 100-percent shadow with a 100-percent dot of the ink, and so on.

To adjust the curve, you can drag points on the curve or enter values in the percentage text boxes.

2 Enter the following values for the different ink percentages:

- Leave 0 in the 0-percent text box.

- Delete the 3 from the 5-percent text box.

- Enter 20 in the 50-percent text box.

- Enter 17 in the 60-percent text box.

- Enter 61 in the 70-percent text box.

- Enter 100 in the 100-percent text box.

Leave all the other text boxes blank.

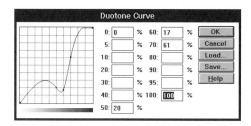

These values lighten the midtones in the image, and distribute more color in the highlights and shadows. For more information about adjusting curves, see the *Adobe Photoshop User Guide*.

3 Click OK in the Duotone Curve dialog box. The adjusted curve appears next to Ink 2 in the Duotone Options dialog box.

4 Click OK to apply the color and ink distribution to the image. The magenta and yellow create a sepia-tone color.

5 Save the image as TPLATE3.PSD in the Projects directory.

CREATING ILLUSTRATIVE EFFECTS

Now you will create some special effects using the duotone and tritone you just created. As you learned in Lesson 4, you can create one type of illustrative effect by *posterizing* the colors. Inverting colors, to create a negative, produces another interesting effect.

To posterize the colors in an image:

1 Activate the DPLATE2.PSD image.

2 Choose Map from the Image menu and Posterize from the submenu.

3 In the Posterize dialog box, enter a value of 6 for Levels and click OK.

This reduces the gray levels in the image from 256 to 6, flattening the image.

4 Save the image as PPLATE2.PSD. You will use this file in the final composite image.

To invert colors:

1 Activate the TPLATE3.PSD image.

2 Choose Map from the Image menu and Invert from the submenu (or press Control+I).

The tritone image is inverted, as if you created a negative of the image.

3 Save the file as IPLATE3.PSD. You will also use this file in the final composite image.

CONVERTING A COLOR IMAGE TO A BITMAPPED IMAGE

To prepare the last part of the composite image, you will convert the PLATE4.PSD image to a bitmapped image, using a pattern. Before converting the file, you must store the pattern you want to use in the pattern buffer.

To convert a color image to a bitmap:

1 Open the INTSUR.EPS file in the LESSON10 directory. Accept the EPS Rasterizer default values and click OK to open the file.

2 Select all of the file, choose Define Pattern from the Edit menu, then close the file.

3 Open the PLATE4.PSD file in the LESSON10 directory.

4 Drag the file down and place it under the PLATE1.PSD file and to the left of the PLATE3.PSD file, with the borders touching.

5 Convert the file to Grayscale mode.

To convert a color image to a bitmapped image, you first must convert it to a grayscale image. This conversion removes the hue and saturation information from the pixels and leaves the brightness values. A bitmapped image treats the 256 levels of gray in a grayscale image as either black (0 to 127) or white (128 to 256).

6 Choose Bitmap from the Mode menu. The Bitmap dialog box appears.

You have a choice of five methods to use when converting a grayscale image to a bitmapped image. These options determine the quality of the new bitmapped image.

7 Leave the resolution at 72, click Custom Pattern under Method, then click OK.

The image is converted to a bitmap using the pattern.

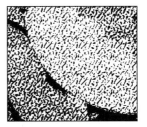

The file size decreases dramatically, to about 5K. Bitmapped images consist of 1 bit of color (black or white) per pixel, and require the least amount of memory. The Channels palette indicates that bitmaps are one-channel images.

8 Save the file as BPLATE4.PSD in the Projects directory.

COMBINING IMAGES INTO A COMPOSITE IMAGE

Now you are ready to combine the four separate images into a composite image.

1 Create a new RGB Color file that is 5.6 inches wide and 4.8 inches high, with a resolution of 72 ppi. Name the file CPLATE1.PSD.

2 Activate the IPLATE1.PSD image.

3 Select all of the file and copy it to the Clipboard.

4 Paste the IPLATE1.PSD image into the CPLATE1.PSD file.

5 Click a selection tool, then drag the image into the upper-left corner of the file.

6 Activate the PPLATE2.PSD image, select, and copy all of it to the Clipboard, then paste it into the upper-right corner of the CPLATE1.PSD file.

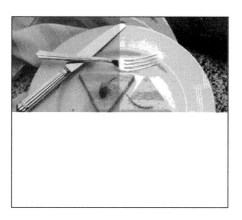

7 Repeat the same process to paste the IPLATE3.PSD image into the lower-right corner of the CPLATE1.PSD image.

8 Convert the BPLATE4.PSD file to Grayscale mode by accepting the default Size Ration of 1, then convert the grayscale image to RGB mode.

You must convert a bitmap image to RGB mode before you can add it to an RGB image. You can't convert a bitmap image directly to RGB; you must first convert it to a grayscale image.

9 Select all of the BPLATE4.PSD image, copy it, and paste it into the lower-left corner to complete the composite image.

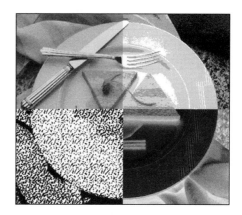

10 Deselect the last selection, then save the file as CPLATE2.PSD.

This image will be used again when you create a poster in Lesson 13.

11 Close the files.

The information in this lesson has only touched on a few of the capabilities of Adobe Photoshop to convert images from one type to another. See the *Adobe Photoshop User Guide* for complete details on all the conversion options.

LE MONDE

B

Gourmet Visions

LESSON 11: PRODUCING COLOR SEPARATIONS AND PRINTING

This lesson provides an overview of basic printing concepts and describes how to print using Adobe Photoshop. The lesson also discusses creating and printing color separations (a *separated image* is one that has been converted from RGB to CMYK mode). Specifically, this lesson explains how Adobe Photoshop converts RGB values to CMYK values.

Calibration ensures that what you see on-screen matches the printed output, and vice versa. For high-resolution printing, it's important to make sure that your system is calibrated correctly before you create or print separations. In Lesson 1, you began the calibration process by entering the default values in the Monitor Setup and Printing Inks Setup dialog boxes. This lesson provides more information on the settings in the Printing Inks Setup dialog box and discusses options in the Separation Setup dialog box. Before separating your own images, you should go through the entire system-calibration process, as detailed in the *Adobe Photoshop User Guide*.

Even if you don't have a printer connected to your computer, you might want to read through the sections on printing, so you understand the Adobe Photoshop printing options. You will then be able to set up your files correctly before sending them to an outside printer.

In this lesson, you'll separate an image (and use a pre-separated image) to learn about the process of color separation. You can then print one or both images. It should take you about an hour to complete this lesson.

In this lesson, you'll learn how to do the following:

• convert an RGB image to a CMYK image for printing

• adjust the color separation for dot gain, black generation, and trap

• print a color composite

• print a four-color separation

• print a selected area of an image

• print a halftone

This lesson uses two versions of the same image, GLASSRGB.PSD and GLASSTRP.PSD, and the Portrait image that you worked with in Lesson 7.

GLASSRGB.PSD   GLASSTRP.PSD

PRGB.PSD   PCMYK.PSD

BEGINNING THIS LESSON

In this lesson, you will separate an image and open several images supplied in both RGB and CMYK mode, so you can compare changes made to the images. The settings in the Printing Inks Setup, Separation Setup, and Separation Tables dialog boxes are critical to creating correct color separations.

PRINTING: AN OVERVIEW

The most common way to output images is to produce a positive or negative image on paper or film, and then transfer the image to a printing plate to be run on a press.

To print continuous-tone images, the image must be broken down into a series of dots. These dots are created when you apply a *halftone screen* to the image. The dots in a halftone screen control how much ink is deposited at a specific location. Varying the size and density of the dots creates the optical illusion of variations of gray or continuous color in the image. In the case of a color printout, four halftone screens are used—cyan, magenta, yellow, and black—one for each ink used in the printing process.

In conventional graphics, a halftone is produced by placing a halftone screen between a piece of film and the image, and then exposing the film. In Adobe Photoshop, you specify the attributes for the halftone screen prior to producing the film or paper output. To achieve the best results, the output device you use, such as a PostScript imagesetter, should be set to the correct density limit, and the processor should be properly calibrated. If these factors are inconsistent, the results can be unpredictable.

To print color separations in Adobe Photoshop, you first convert the RGB image to CMYK, and then adjust how the various plates are generated

(and, if necessary, correct for trap). After setting the other print options, you print the four images used for color separations (one image for each of the process colors).

Adobe Photoshop also lets you print an image as a grayscale halftone, as a composite image, or as individual channels.

PRODUCING A COLOR SEPARATION

Producing a color separation is the process of converting an RGB image to a CMYK image. The conversion splits the RGB colors into the four process colors: cyan, magenta, yellow, and black.

As you learned in Lesson 10, when Adobe Photoshop converts an RGB image to CMYK, it converts the RGB color values to Lab mode, builds a color table, and then references the table to complete the conversion to CMYK mode.

The information in the Monitor Setup dialog box is used for the first step of conversion (converting the RGB color values to Lab values). The information in the Printing Inks Setup and Separation Setup dialog boxes is used to build the color table. During the RGB–Lab–CMYK conversion, the program refers to the color table values to calculate the correct CMYK values for each Lab pixel. The program then converts the image to CMYK mode.

Once in CMYK mode, the program must reconvert the color values to RGB so that the image can be displayed on an RGB monitor. To do this, Adobe Photoshop converts the CMYK values back to Lab (using the same color table if no values in Printing Inks Setup and Separation Setup have been changed) and then back to RGB (again using the Monitor Setup information).

Separating an image

To demonstrate how separation works, you'll separate the GLASSRGB.PSD image using the default separation options, and then compare the RGB color with its CMYK equivalents.

To separate the image:

1 Open the GLASSRGB.PSD image in the LESSON11 directory.

2 Choose CMYK Color from the Mode menu to convert the RGB image to CMYK mode.

The program builds a color table, using the information in the Printing Inks Setup and the Separation Setup dialog boxes, and then converts the image.

3 Save the file as GLASSCMY.PSD in the Projects directory.

4 Make sure the Brushes, Channels, Colors, and Info palettes are open or collapsed on your screen.

5 Choose Preferences from the File menu and General from the submenu.

6 Click to deselect Color Channels in Color under Display and click OK.

To compare how the color has been separated:

1 Reopen the GLASSRGB.PSD image.

2 Drag the GLASSRGB.PSD image to the right until it is next to the GLASSCMY.PSD image.

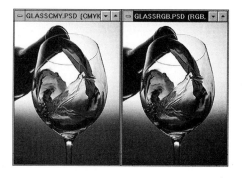

You shouldn't see any difference between the two images. As with most scanned images, all the colors in the original RGB image were within the CMYK gamut, and didn't need to be changed. If the image had contained colors outside the CMYK gamut, the RGB colors would have been converted to their nearest CMYK equivalents. You'll see an example of this in a minute.

Displaying the individual channels

Each channel for the image displays the color information for one color component. It is the amount of each color of ink deposited at any point on the paper (and how much of the ink is absorbed) that determines the final printed color. To see how the channels will look when they are printed, you're going to display the channels individually.

To preview the printing of individual channels:

1 With the GLASSRGB.PSD window active, click Red in the Channels palette.

The channel appears in grayscale. This is how the channel will print. Darker gray areas indicate where more color appears; lighter gray areas indicate less color.

2 Display the green and blue channels to see their color distribution, then return to the composite channel.

3 Activate the GLASSCMY.PSD window.

The Channels palette now shows channels for the cyan, magenta, yellow, and black colors.

4 Display each of the four process color channels.

You can see how each plate contributes to the overall color in the final image.

5 Close the GLASSCMY.PSD image.

Converting out-of-gamut colors

Most scanned photographs contain RGB colors within the CMYK gamut, and all the colors are converted with no substitution when you change the image to CMYK mode. Images that were created or altered digitally, however, often contain RGB colors that are out of gamut. You were introduced to the idea of out-of-gamut colors in Lesson 7. As you may remember, out-of-gamut colors are indicated in the Colors palette, the Color Picker, and the Info palette by an exclamation mark.

When separating an RGB image, Adobe Photoshop converts colors that are out of the CMYK gamut to their closest CMYK equivalents. The conversion allows you to print the colors. To see how this works, you're going to add a gradient to the GLASSRGB.PSD image that contains an out-of-gamut color.

To convert out-of-gamut colors:

1 Make the GLASSRGB.PSD image active and be sure you are in the RGB composite channel.

2 Click the bright blue swatch in the first row of the Colors palette (the fifth swatch from the left) to set the foreground color for the gradient.

An alert triangle appears under the color selection boxes in the Colors palette, indicating that this blue can't be reproduced as a CMYK color. The swatch next to the triangle shows the closest CMYK equivalent to the color.

The first six swatches in the Colors palette are mixes of pure RGB colors and are out of gamut; they cannot be displayed or printed as CMYK equivalents. If you plan to separate an RGB image, it's a good idea to try not to use pure RGB colors.

3 Set the background color to white as the ending color for the gradient.

4 Click the gradient tool.

5 In the Brushes palette, set the Opacity to 100 percent and choose Darken from the Mode pop-up menu.

6 Starting at the top of the image, drag the gradient tool down about 1-1/2 inches. The blend appears.

7 Convert the GLASSRGB.PSD image to CMYK Color mode.

The color conversion of the blend with the out-of-gamut color occurs automatically. The royal blue in the RGB image appears as violet blue in the CMYK image. The violet blue in the CMYK image is the printable equivalent of the RGB royal blue.

8 To compare the colors, choose Undo to switch between the RGB blend and the CMYK blend.

9 Close the GLASSRGB.PSD image without saving changes.

CUSTOMIZING SEPARATION OPTIONS

As you know, the separation of an image is controlled by the settings in the Monitor Setup, Printing Inks Setup, Separation Setup, and Separation Tables dialog boxes. An important concept to keep in mind is that these options do not affect RGB images. *They affect image data only when you convert the file from RGB to CMYK mode.* Therefore, if you convert an image to CMYK and then change the calibration settings, you must reconvert the image to CMYK for the changes to take effect. Because of this interaction between settings and conversions, you can choose to use one of two strategies for creating color separations.

Working in RGB mode

One way to create color separations is to work in RGB mode, set the separation preferences to compensate for conditions on-press, and then convert the image to CMYK mode. During the conversion, Adobe Photoshop changes the image to compensate for the settings you have made. When converted to CMYK, the image appears the same on the screen as the original RGB image. The advantage to working in RGB is that it is faster than working in CMYK mode. The disadvantage is that you may need to track your colors more carefully to note out-of-gamut colors.

Working in CMYK mode

The second strategy for creating color separations is to print a color proof to show the needed corrections, then work in CMYK mode as you make color corrections until the screen display matches the desired output. The display will change and you will see the colors that will print. Working in CMYK mode is slower than working in RGB mode.

When you work in CMYK mode and set separation settings, such as dot gain, the CMYK display changes to *simulate* the settings and show how the image will appear when printed. For example, if you enter a dot gain of 30 percent while your image is in CMYK mode, the image will appear darker on the screen to approximate what the image would look like when printed on a press under those conditions. However, the actual image is not changed. (In contrast, the RGB image is altered when you convert it to CMYK mode.)

Adjusting the printing inks setup

In this part of the lesson, you'll experiment with different separation preferences to compare their effects. Two options that clearly illustrate the difference in separation settings are *dot gain* (in the Printing Inks Setup dialog box) and *black generation* (in the Separation Setup dialog box).

To adjust for printing inks and paper:

1 Open the PCMYK.PSD file in the LESSON11 directory.

You probably remember this image from Lesson 7. It's been resized for use in this lesson. The PCMYK.PSD image was separated using the default settings in the Monitor Setup, Printing Inks Setup, Separation Setup, and Separation Tables dialog boxes.

2 Choose Preferences from the File menu and Printing Inks Setup from the submenu.

3 Make sure SWOP (Coated) is chosen in the Ink Colors pop-up menu in the Printing Inks Setup dialog box.

SWOP (standard web offset proofing) ink is the default ink color. Coated paper is also the default setting. This is the same setting used to separate the PCMYK.PSD image. By choosing the same ink, you'll be able to clearly see the difference caused by changing the dot gain.

When you're producing your own proofs, you typically obtain the ink type and dot gain information from the print shop that will be printing your final job, or you choose your own printer from the Ink Colors list.

4 Enter a dot gain of 30 percent.

Dot gain is a printing characteristic that causes dots to be printed larger than they should be, producing darker tones or color than expected. Different printers and papers have different dot gains. The default dot gain for SWOP is 20 percent, and this was the value used to separate the PCMYK.PSD image.

5 Click OK.

Adobe Photoshop builds a new color table using the dot gain setting you changed in the Printing Inks Setup dialog box. The CMYK image version now appears substantially darker, simulating what your image would look like if it were printed using a 30-percent dot gain. Remember that only the display has changed, *not* the actual CMYK image.

6 Choose Undo to compare the effect of the default dot gain of 20 percent with that of the 30-percent dot gain you just applied.

In the Printing Inks Setup dialog box, try choosing other options from the Ink Colors pop-up menu and note how the default dot-gain settings for the inks or printers vary.

7 Reset the options to the defaults of SWOP (Coated) ink color and 20-percent dot gain, then click OK.

Adjusting the black generation and undercolor removal

Because of impurities in all printing inks, a mix of the process colors yields a muddy brown instead of a pure black. To compensate for this deficiency, printers remove some cyan, magenta, and yellow in areas where the three colors overlap, and add black ink. There are two *styles* of removing or replacing color when converting RGB color to CMYK color: undercolor removal (UCR) or gray component replacement (GCR), also known as *black generation*. You will use the file you have open now, and an RGB version of the same image, to compare black-generation settings.

To adjust the black generation:

1 Open the PRGB.PSD image in the LESSON11 directory and drag the image to the right so that it is side by side with the PCMYK.PSD image.

2 With the PRGB.PSD image active, choose Preferences from the File menu and Separation Setup from the submenu. The Separation Setup dialog box appears.

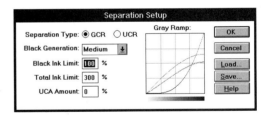

The dialog box displays a graph showing how the neutral colors in the image (that is, colors with equal parts of cyan, magenta, and yellow—sometimes called a *gray ramp*) separate given the current values of the Separation Setup parameters. The x-axis represents the neutral color value, from 0 percent (white) to 100 percent (black). The y-axis represents the amount of each ink that will be generated for the given value.

3 If necessary, click GCR.

This is the default option, used for coated stock. In GCR replacement, more black ink is used over a wider range of colors. GCR separations tend to reproduce dark, saturated colors and maintain gray balance better on-press than UCR separations. You would choose UCR if you were printing on uncoated stock or newsprint.

4 Choose Maximum from the Black Generation pop-up menu.

Notice that the ramp changes to show the new distribution of ink.

5 Click OK to close the dialog box.

6 Convert the PRGB.PSD image to CMYK Color mode.

As with the Printing Inks Setup dialog box, Adobe Photoshop builds a new color table whenever you change a setting in the Separation Setup dialog box.

7 Compare the two images.

You probably can't see much of a difference even though the original CMYK image on the left was converted using the default Medium black-generation setting, and the image on the right used the Maximum setting. To better see the effect of black generation, you're going to compare the black channels in each image.

8 Click Black in the Channels palette to display the black channel for each image.

The separation on the left (the original CMYK image) appears lighter than the separation on the right (the converted image).

9 Use the eyedropper to sample the background along the left edge of each image. (Make sure that the window is active before trying to use the eyedropper.)

In the left image (converted using the Medium setting), the K values in the Info palette range from about 81 percent at the bottom of the image to 89 percent at the top. In the right image (converted using the Maximum setting), the K values range from about 91 percent at the bottom of the image to 96 percent at the top.

10 Close both files without saving any changes.

Creating trap

Trap is the overlap needed to ensure that a slight misalignment or movement of the plates while printing does not affect the final appearance of the printed image. Adobe Photoshop uses the trap setting to determine how far overlapping colors should be spread outward to compensate for misregistration on-press. Overprinting colors slightly to prevent tiny gaps from appearing in the printed image is known as adding traps.

Adobe Photoshop traps only by spreading; it does not choke colors. (A *spread trap* overlaps a lighter object onto a darker background. A *choke trap* does the opposite, overlapping a lighter background onto a darker object.) See the *Adobe Photoshop User Guide* for more information on the standard rules for trapping.

Most photos, unless they contain solid tints or letterforms, do not need to be trapped.

To add traps:

1 Open the GLASSTRP.PSD file.

In this image, distinctly different colors in the logo and surrounding areas touch and need to be trapped.

2 Zoom in to a 4:1 view of the image to see how the color spreads.

Especially in the thinner stroke of the *V*, you can see how the yellow blends with the blue background. The blending is a result of the magenta and yellow in the letters spreading out underneath the dark blue. In Adobe Photoshop, lighter colors spread under darker colors. This means that yellow spreads under cyan, magenta, and black.

3 Choose Trap from the Image menu, enter a value of 4, and click OK.

This causes the yellow to spread too much under the darker blue, as you can clearly see around the edges of the logo.

4 Choose Undo to return to the original image, choose Trap again, enter 1 in the dialog box, then click OK.

This amount of trap improves the letters and also causes a slight darkening in the high-contrast and shadow areas, especially near the top of the wineglass stem. This subtle effect is hard to see in the composite view of the image, but shows up clearly if you look at the yellow channel.

5 Click Yellow in the Channels palette to display the yellow channel, then press Control+Z to undo and redo the trapping so you can see the effect.

Yellow channel before trap *Yellow channel after trap*

6 Save this image as GLASST1.PSD in the Projects directory.

7 Close the file.

SELECTING PRINTING OPTIONS

Before you begin preparation for printing, make sure that you are properly connected to the printer you will be printing to and that it is turned on.

To select printing options, you first make choices from the Page Setup dialog box, then choose options from the Print dialog box.

The Page Setup dialog box lets you print labels, crop marks, calibration bars, registration marks, and negatives. You can also print emulsion-side down, and using interpolation (for PostScript Level 2 printers).

Referencing the Help file

Included in Adobe Photoshop is the ability to reference the Help file for information on Photoshop tasks, tools and options. You may find the Help file useful to find detailed information on questions you may have. You will now use the Help file to get more information on printing.

To use the Help file:

1 Choose Glossary from the Help menu.

2 Click the Search button and type **Printing**.

3 Double-click the selected word Printing in the scroll dialog, below the word Printing that you typed in.

Topics related to printing appear in the scroll box .

4 Click on the topic Print Command and click Go To.

The Print Command information appears.

5 Browse through this document until you are finished reading the Print Command information.

6 In the Photoshop Help window choose Exit from the File menu.

See the *Adobe Photoshop Help* file for more helpful information on other topics.

SPECIFYING SETTINGS FOR DIFFERENT IMAGE TYPES

The type of image you're printing, and the type of output you want, determine which selections you make in the Page Setup and the Print dialog boxes.

Printing a color composite

A color composite is a single print that superimposes the red, green, and blue channels of an RGB image (or the cyan, magenta, yellow, and black channels of a CMYK image). For your first printing task, you're going to add a name to the image as you print an RGB file.

1 Open the PRGB.PSD file.

2 Choose Page Setup from the File menu.

3 Click the Caption button. The Caption dialog box appears.

4 Type your name in the caption box, then click OK.

5 Click OK to close the Page Setup dialog box.

6 Display the page preview box.

A small gray box indicates the location of the caption. All of the settings you make in the Page Setup dialog box can be previewed before printing.

7 Choose Print from the File menu. The Print dialog box appears.

8 Select the Print as RGB option.

This option tells the printer to produce color output. If you choose Gray, the file prints as a black-and-white image. If you choose CMYK, Photoshop will print a CMYK version of an RGB, Lab, or indexed color image.

9 Click OK to print the file as a composite.

Printing a color-corrected version of an RGB or Lab image

You can print a color-corrected version of RGB, Lab, and indexed color images (if you're working with an indexed color image, convert the image to RGB before printing). This option allows Adobe Photoshop to make an on-the-fly conversion to CMYK colors for the RGB or Lab file, and usually produces better results than a print shop. The option works with color PostScript and Quick-Draw printers, but is not recommended for PostScript Level 2 printers. Before using the CMYK option, make sure that you have entered the correct settings in the Printing Inks Setup dialog box.

To print a color-corrected version of this image:

1 Choose Print from the File menu.

2 Click the Print in CMYK option in the Print dialog box, then click OK.

Adobe Photoshop prints the color-corrected image.

3 Close the file without saving changes.

Printing a separated image

By default, a single document is printed for CMYK images. You can choose to print the four separations for an image.

To print a separated image:

1 Open the PCMYK.PSD image.

2 Choose Print from the File menu.

3 Select the Print Separations option to print the file as four separations, then click OK.

The image prints as four separate pieces of paper or film. If this option is not selected, the CMYK image prints as a composite image.

4 Close the file without saving changes.

To print a selected area:

1 Activate the GLASST1.PSD image located in the Projects directory.

2 Select the logo using the rectangular marquee tool. The rectangular marquee tool is the only selection tool you can use when choosing an area to be printed.

3 Choose Print from the File menu.

4 Click the Selection option under Print Range.

5 If necessary, deselect the Print Separations option to print a composite.

6 Click OK to print the logo.

7 Choose None from the Select Menu.

Printing a halftone

To print an image with a halftone screen, you use the Halftone Screen option in the Page Setup dialog box. The results of using a halftone screen are apparent only in the printed copy; you don't see the halftone screen in the monitor display. Your computer must be connected to a printer before you can set up the halftone screen.

You use one halftone screen to print a grayscale image. You use four halftone screens (one for each color) to print color separations. In this example, you'll be adjusting the screen frequency and dot shape to produce a halftone screen for a grayscale image.

The *screen frequency* controls the density of dots on the screen. Since the dots are arranged in lines on the screen, the common measurement for screen frequency is lines per inch (lpi). The higher the screen frequency, the finer the image produced. Magazines, for example, tend to use fine screens of 133 lpi and higher because they are usually printed on coated paper stock on high-quality presses. Newspapers, which are usually printed on lower-quality paper stock, tend to use lower screen frequencies, such as 85-lpi screens.

The *screen angle* used to create halftones of grayscale images is generally 45 degrees. For color separations, you specify an angle for each of the color screens. Setting the screens at different angles ensures that the dots placed by the four screens blend to look like continuous color and do not produce moiré patterns.

Diamond-shaped dots are most commonly used in halftone screens. In Adobe Photoshop, however, you can also choose round, elliptical, linear, square, and cross-shaped dots.

To set up the halftone screen:

1 Convert the GLASST1.PSD image to Grayscale mode.

2 Choose Page Setup from the File menu.

3 Click the Screen button. The Halftone Screens dialog box appears.

4 Enter 80 in the Frequency box and make sure that lines/inch is chosen from the measurement pop-up menu.

5 Leave Angle at the default setting of 45 degrees.

6 Choose Ellipse from the Shape pop-up menu.

7 Click OK to produce the screen.

To print the halftone:

1 If necessary, select a printer and click OK.

2 Choose Print from the File menu, then click OK to print the file.

3 Close the file. If you want to, you can save the grayscale version of this file.

This completes your introduction to producing color separations and printing using Adobe Photoshop. This is a very complex and rapidly changing area of digital technology, and you should be proud of what you've done in this lesson. For a more complete discussion of calibration, color separation, and all the printing options, see the *Adobe Photoshop User Guid*e or the *Photoshop Help* menu.

Gourmet Visions

LESSON 12: IMPORTING AND EXPORTING FILES

This lesson explains how you open (or import) and save (or export) files that are not in the Adobe Photoshop format. So far, you've been working with Adobe Photoshop 2.5 files. Adobe Photoshop also allows you to open files in Photoshop 2.0, Amiga IFF, BMP, EPS, GIF, JPEG, MacPaint, PCX, PIXAR, PixelPaint, Raw, Scitex™ CT, Targa, and TIFF files. In addition, Adobe Photoshop opens files scanned using the TWAIN interface, and opens and decompresses EPS files saved using EPS JPEG compression.

You can save Adobe Photoshop files in most of these same file formats, plus one additional format—Amiga HAM. Using export modules, you can also save EPS files using JPEG compression, export files for printing on a color dot matrix printer, and export paths to Adobe Illustrator.

You can open Kodak® PhotoCD files in Adobe Photoshop and manipulate the files just like any other digitized images. You must enter a resolution and file format when you open the files. If you open the file in Lab format, all the color information is preserved. You cannot save files in the PhotoCD format from Adobe Photoshop. See the *Adobe Photoshop User Guide* or the *Photoshop Help* menu for more information about using PhotoCD files.

If these file types aren't familiar to you, don't worry. All you need to know is that Adobe Photoshop can open almost any file you might want to use in an image, and can save your files in the formats commonly used by other applications.

In most cases, opening and saving non-Adobe Photoshop files is as simple as using the standard Open As and Save As dialog boxes. The different file formats appear in a pop-up menu in the dialog boxes, and you choose the format you want to open or save in. For a few file types, you import files using commands in the Acquire menu and export files using commands in the Export menu. Sometimes, opening and saving files requires an additional dialog box. These dialog boxes are described in detail in the *Adobe Photoshop User Guide.*

This lesson shows you how to use Adobe Photoshop and Adobe Illustrator in tandem. If you don't have Adobe Illustrator, you can skip the part of the lesson in which you create Adobe Illustrator artwork. The finished Adobe Illustrator file is included with the *Classroom in a Book* files. It should take you about 30 minutes to complete this lesson.

In this lesson, you'll learn how to do the following:

• open and save JPEG files

• save in EPS format

• export a path to Adobe Illustrator

• create type that follows a path in Adobe Illustrator

• place Adobe Illustrator art in an Adobe Photoshop file

At the end of this lesson you'll have a tempting advertisement that invites Gourmet Visions customers to sample the pleasure of fresh sushi.

Source file (SUSHI.PSD)

Source file (TYPE.EPS)

Source file (TYPEBAR.EPS)

Ending image (SUSHIAD.PSD)

BEGINNING THIS LESSON

In this lesson, you will open a beginning image and a reference file. Both of these files are in CMYK mode. You'll work directly in the CMYK mode for this lesson. In order to see some of the effects of saving on a file's size, you'll open the files in this lesson from the LESSON12 directory window.

To begin this lesson:

1 Make sure that the Paths palette and Brushes palette are open or collapsed on your screen (you can hide or close the other Adobe Photoshop palettes).

2 Open the SUSHI.PSD and the SUSHIAD.PSD files in the LESSON12 directory.

UNDERSTANDING COMPRESSION

Compressing a file can save large amounts of space on your storage disk, without noticeably affecting the quality of the image. When you're working with very large files, compression is especially important since graphic files can easily exceed 10 MB in size. (To understand how big these files are, think of how much information you store on your hard disk. If you have an 80-MB hard disk, you can store only eight 10-MB graphic files.)

There are several compression types. Adobe Photoshop allows you to save or compress files using the Joint Photographic Experts Group (JPEG) format. JPEG compression economizes on the way data is stored and also identifies and discards *extra* data—that is, information the human eye cannot see. Because data is discarded or lost, JPEG is referred to as *lossy* compression. With lossy compression, an image that is compressed and then decompressed is not identical to the original image. In most cases, the difference between the original and the compressed version of the image is indistinguishable.

SAVING A FILE IN JPEG FORMAT

Currently, the SUSHI.PSD file is in Adobe Photoshop 2.5 format. You are going to reduce the file size of this image by saving it in JPEG format.

To save a file in JPEG format:

1 Activate the SUSHI.PSD image.

The size preview box indicates that the current file size is 578K.

2 Choose Save As from the File menu.

3 Make sure the name of this file reads SUSHI.JPG and select your Projects directory.

JPEG lets you choose from three compression settings. In general, an image compressed using the Excellent option has a compression ratio of between 5:1 and 15:1. The higher the quality setting, the less the file is compressed and the less the file size is reduced.

4 Choose JPEG (*.JPG) from the Save File as Format Type pop-up menu at the bottom of the dialog box and click OK.

The JPEG Options dialog box appears.

5 Move the slider to the Good setting and click Save.

6 Close the file.

7 Choose Open from the File menu and select SUSHI.JPG in the Open dialog box. Notice that using the Good setting reduced the file size from 578K to about 75K (the file size is shown in the lower right corner).

8 Click OK to reopen the SUSHI.JPG file.

Note that the size preview box shows the original file size of 578K. This is because the file is decompressed as it is opened. This decompression is done automatically by Adobe Photoshop whenever you open a file saved in JPEG format.

9 Close the file once more. You will not be using the JPEG file again in this lesson.

SAVING A FILE IN EPS FORMAT

The Encapsulated PostScript (EPS) file format is supported by most illustration and page-layout programs. In order to use Adobe Photoshop images with these kinds of applications, you must save them as EPS files.

Follow these steps *very closely* in order to continue the procedures through step 2 on page 188.

To save a file in EPS format:

1 Open the original SUSHI.PSD file (not the JPEG-compressed version) in the LESSON12 directory.

2 Choose Save As from the File menu.

3 Choose EPS from the Save File as Format Type pop-up menu.

4 Make sure the name of this file reads SUSHI.EPS and select your Projects directory and click OK.

The EPS Format dialog box appears. There are several options available when you save a file in EPS format. The *Adobe Photoshop User Guide* explains these options. For this file, you're going to use the default values.

5 Make sure the Preview option is set to 8-bit IBM PC, the Encoding option is set to Binary, and the Desktop Color Separation option is Off, then click OK.

The Binary option creates a file that is about half the size of a file saved with the ASCII option and takes half as long to transfer to the printer. However, some applications (such as Aldus PageMaker and FreeHand) might not support binary EPS documents. When you're going to use these applications, use the ASCII encoding option.

EXPORTING A PATH TO ADOBE ILLUSTRATOR

For the final image, you're going to create a path in this EPS file, export the path to an Adobe Illustrator file, then use the path to determine the placement of the type. Just for practice, create and export the path even if you won't be working in Adobe Illustrator.

To export a path to Adobe Illustrator:

1 Use the pen tool in the Paths palette to draw a path around the plate. Place the first anchor point in the top center of the plate.

Drag the points to draw the curved outline. Be sure to close the path. Your path should look something like the following illustration. Feel free to use the Arrow tool and to edit the path.

2 Choose Save Path from the Paths palette pop-up menu and name the path *Plate*, and click OK.

3 Choose Export from the File menu and Paths from the submenu. The Export paths to file dialog box appears.

Make sure the path file name appears as follows:

PHOTOSHP\PHSCIB\PROJECTS\SUSHI.EPS

4 Click OK.

5 Choose Save from the File menu to save the path with the SUSHI.EPS file.

USING A PATH IN ADOBE ILLUSTRATOR

Now you're ready to use this path in an Adobe Illustrator file. If you don't have Adobe Illustrator, you can read through the following steps or skip to the "Placing Adobe Illustrator Files" section, later in this lesson.

The steps in this section assume you're using Adobe Illustrator 4.0 Windows version or higher.

If you don't have enough memory to open both applications simultaneously, exit Adobe Photoshop for now.

The first thing you're going to do is display the path and the EPS file in Adobe Illustrator.

To use the path in Adobe Illustrator:

1 Open Adobe Illustrator. A blank untitled window appears.

2 Choose Open from the File menu (or press Control+O) and select the SUSHI.EPS file from the Projects directory (this is your exported path file).

The path appears in the window. The crop marks indicate the size of the Adobe Photoshop image.

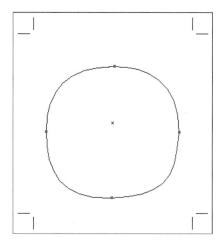

3 Choose the Selection tool (top tool in the toolbox).

4 Click the path to select it.

Notice you can alter the path if you need to.

Adding type in Adobe Illustrator

Now you're ready to add the type. The top of the path is going to serve as the defining border of the type. In Adobe Illustrator this is called *path type* (as opposed to *area type*, which is like the type you can enter in Adobe Photoshop).

To create the type:

1 Select the path-type tool. The path-type tool is adjacent to the type tool in the toolbox.

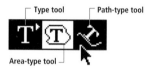

The path-type tool makes the type you enter follow the curve of the path. When you move into the image area, the insertion point appears with a curved line running through it.

2 Click the anchor point at the top center of the path to display the insertion point, then type **Kyoto Sushi**.

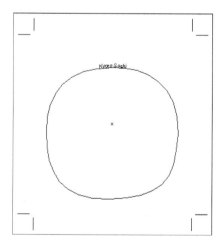

The type appears along the path. This type is in the default font of 12-point Helvetica. (If you don't see any type, you might need to install this font.)

3 Choose Alignment from the Type menu and Centered from the submenu (or press Control+Shift+T).

Setting the type attributes

Now you're ready to set the attributes for the type. In Adobe Illustrator, unlike in Adobe Photoshop, you can enter the type first and then set the type attributes.

To set the type attributes:

1 Choose Select All from the Edit menu (or press Control+A).

2 Choose Type Style from the Type menu (or press Control+T). The Type Style dialog box appears.

3 Type 48 for Size and click Apply, then be sure to click OK.

You can type in the font and size or choose them from the pop-up menus. As you change options in the Type Style dialog box, click the Apply button to reflect the new settings.

4 Choose Tracking/Kerning from the Type menu (or press Control+Shift+K).

When you choose this command, the Tracking dialog box appears. Tracking creates uniform spacing in type.

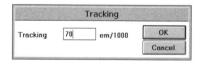

5 Enter 70 in the Tracking text box and press OK.

As a final adjustment, you're going to increase the tracking in the second word.

6 Click outside the type to deselect it, then double-click the word to select only *Sushi*.

7 Choose Tracking/Kerning from the Type menu.

8 Enter 100 in the Tracking dialog box and press OK.

9 Click the selection tool (the arrow pointer in the upper-left corner of the toolbox), and drag the top of the I-beam to center the type along the top of the path.

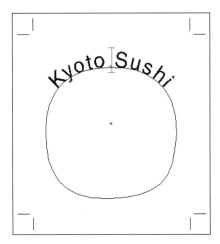

Changing the type color

Currently, the type appears in black around the top of the path. You want the type to be white in your final Adobe Photoshop image.

To change the type color:

1 Select the path-type tool and click anywhere in the type to display the insertion point.

2 Choose Select All from the Edit menu.

3 Choose Paint Style from the Paint menu (or press Control+I). The Paint Style dialog box appears.

4 Click White under Fill and click OK.

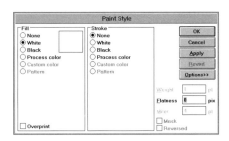

5 Choose Save As from the File menu. The Save As dialog box appears.

6 Name the file TYPE1.EPS, set the Preview option to Color and leave the default setting for Compatibility, then save the file in the Projects directory.

7 Choose Exit from the File menu to quit Adobe Illustrator.

If you want to learn more about using Adobe Illustrator, see the *Classroom in a Book* package available for Adobe Illustrator.

PLACING ADOBE ILLUSTRATOR FILES

To complete your advertisement, you're going to bring two Adobe Illustrator files into your Adobe Photoshop image. One file is a design element that includes the Japanese name for Kyoto Sushi. The other is the type file (either the one you just created or the file included in the LESSON12 directory).

When you want to use an Adobe Illustrator file as a new Adobe Photoshop document, you open the file using the Open command. In this case, you want to include the files in an existing Adobe Photoshop file, so you use the Place command.

To place the EPS files in the Adobe Photoshop image:

1 Return to the original SUSHI.PSD file in Adobe Photoshop. (This is the Photoshop 2.5 file.)

If you quit Adobe Photoshop when you started Adobe Illustrator, launch Adobe Photoshop to start the program, then open the SUSHI.PSD image, and the SUSHIAD.PSD image.

2 Choose Place from the File menu. The Place dialog box appears.

3 Select the TYPEBAR.EPS file in the LESSON12 directory, and click OK.

The red bar with Japanese type appears as a floating selection inside a rectangular box in the center of the image.

4 Click with the gavel to confirm the placement of the bar file.

5 Click a selection tool, drag the bar to the lower-right corner, and position it as shown in the SUSHIAD.PSD file.

6 Choose the Place command again, select the TYPE.EPS file in LESSON12 (or the TYPE1.EPS file in the Projects directory—if you created it in Adobe Illustrator) and click OK.

The placement of the type should be correct.

If you want to change the placement, drag a corner handle to resize the box. Hold down the Shift key as you drag to keep the same aspect ratio as the original Adobe Illustrator file.

7 Click with the gavel to confirm the placement.

8 If necessary, use the arrow keys to reposition the type. (The type should still be a floating selection).

CHANGING THE TYPE OPACITY

This imported type is now the same as any type you create in Adobe Photoshop and can be edited using the standard commands and tools. As a final touch to this image, you're going to change the opacity of the type.

To change the type opacity:

1 Type 8 to set the Opacity in the Brushes palette to 80 percent.

2 Hide the edges of the selection to view the effect.

You can see that the type is less distinct from the background.

3 Experiment with the Opacity slider to see the effect of decreasing or increasing opacity.

4 Save this file as SUSHI1.PSD in the Projects directory.

And that's how easy it is to use other file types with Adobe Photoshop. This lesson showed you just one example of how you can use Adobe Photoshop with other file types and applications. You'll probably discover many other uses for the extensive file types you can import from and export to as you're using Adobe Photoshop in your own work.

LE MONDE

B

Gourmet Visions

Lesson

13

LESSON 13: REVIEW PROJECT— TRADE SHOW POSTER

I n this lesson, you'll have a chance to review what's been covered in Lessons 10, 11, and 12. There are also a few tried-and-true procedures from earlier lessons that should be second-hand to you by now. Hopefully, as you complete this final lesson in *Classroom in a Book*, you'll begin to see how you can put what you've learned to work in your own image creation and editing.

As in the earlier review projects, this lesson provides all the step-by-step instructions you need to complete the project. Detailed explanations, however, are not included. If you need to brush up on specifics, or can't remember how to do something, refer back to the earlier lessons. For a quick reference to the specific topics covered in each lesson, see the table of contents at the beginning of the book.

In Lesson 10, you learned how to convert images from one mode to another, and in Lesson 11, you prepared a color separation for printing. Lesson 12 explained how to open and save in different formats and how to use Adobe Photoshop in conjunction with Adobe Illustrator. In this lesson, you'll use the composite plate you created in Lesson 10 as the main element in a trade show poster. You will then add type to the poster and prepare it for printing. If you have a color printer, you can print out the results. It should take you about half an hour to complete this lesson.

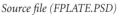
Source file (FPLATE.PSD)

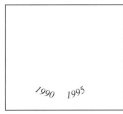
Source file (DATE.EPS)

Ending image (CPOSTER.PSD)

BEGINNING THIS LESSON

As you have done several times before, you will create a new file in this lesson and then copy components from other files into the new image.

To begin the lesson:

1 Open the CPOSTER.PSD file in the LESSON13 directory, zoom out, then resize the window and move this reference file to the upper-right corner of your screen.

2 Create a new RGB Color file that is 310 pixels wide and 400 pixels high with a resolution of 72.

If necessary, use the pop-up menu in the New dialog box to set the units of measurement to pixels before creating the file.

3 Turn on the rulers in the untitled window.

4 Have the Brushes, Colors, Channels, Paths, and Info palettes available (they can be open or collapsed).

CREATING FIXED-SIZE RECTANGLES

To begin creating this poster, you need to draw and fill the blocks for the background.

To create the background:

1 Create a fixed rectangular marquee that is 155 pixels wide and 200 pixels high.

2 Click anywhere in the window to display the marquee and drag it to the upper-left corner. Use the arrow keys to place the marquee flush against the edges of the window.

3 Mix a foreground color in the Colors palette with an R value of about 36, a G value of about 46, and a B value of about 118.

As an alternative, you can use the eyedropper to sample this color from the upper-left quadrant of the final image.

4 Use the paint bucket tool to fill the rectangle.

5 Set the foreground color to black.

6 Use the fixed marquee to create a selection in the lower-right corner of the window, then use the paint bucket tool to fill the rectangle with black.

7 Save the file as CPOST1.PSD in the Projects directory.

Make sure the File Format is Photoshop.

COPYING A SELECTION FROM ANOTHER IMAGE

The first element you'll add to the poster is the composite plate you created in Lesson 10.

To copy the plate:

1 Open the FPLATE.PSD file in the LESSON13 directory (or your version of the final plate from Lesson 10).

The file in the LESSON13 directory has a saved selection that is the outline of the plate. If you're using your file from Lesson 10, you will need to select the plate and save it as a selection.

2 Load the selection and copy it to the Clipboard, then close the FPLATE.PSD image.

3 Paste the selection into the CPOST1.PSD file.

4 Select the rectangular marquee tool.

5 Drag the plate to the center of the window. Line up the four sections of the plate with the background quadrants to position the plate exactly in the center of the image.

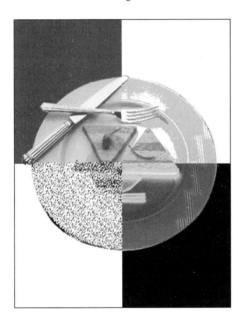

6 Save this selection in channel 4 and name it *Plate* (you will use it again later in this lesson).

7 Save the file.

INVERTING A COLOR SELECTION

The two rectangles behind the California Cuisine type in this image are inverted versions of each other. You'll add these rectangles now and enter the type.

To create the type rectangles:

1 Use a fixed marquee to create a rectangle that is 255 pixels wide and 40 pixels high.

2 Choose Options from the Info palette and change the Ruler Units for the mouse coordinates to inches.

The rulers are displayed in inches in the CPOST1.PSD window.

3 Click to display the marquee and place the rectangle about a quarter-inch from the top of the window and about three-eighths of an inch from the edges of the window.

If you moved the background as well as the marquee, you probably forgot to hold down the Control and Alt keys before you began dragging the selection marquee.

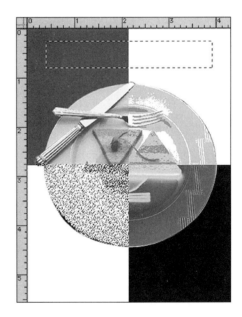

4 Choose Map from the Image menu and Invert from the submenu.

The left side of the rectangle becomes tan and the right side of the rectangle becomes black. When you invert a color selection, its complementary color (on the color wheel) is produced.

5 Deselect the rectangle.

ADDING THE TYPE

Now you're ready to add the California Cuisine type.

To add the type:

1 Click the type tool and click the insertion point in the tan half of the rectangle.

2 Set the font to Helvetica Bold, the Size to 10 points, and the Spacing to 4. Type **CALIFORNIA** (in all caps) in the text box and click OK.

3 Type 10 on the keyboard to set the Brushes palette to 100%.

4 Turn off the edges of the selection and center the type in the tan box.

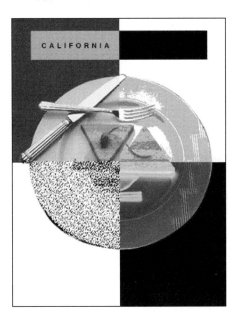

5 Deselect the type.

6 Switch the foreground and background colors so the foreground is white.

7 Click the type tool and click the insertion point in the black half of the rectangle.

8 Set the font to Times Bold Italic, the Size to 12, and the spacing to 10. Type **Cuisine** (upper and lower case) in the text box and click OK.

9 Make sure the Brushes palette opacity reads 100%.

10 Use the arrow keys to center the *Cuisine* type and align it with the *California* type.

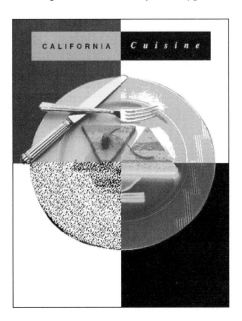

11 Deselect the type and save the file as CPOST2.PSD.

SAVING THE SELECTION AS A PATH

In earlier lessons, you saved a path as a selection so you could reuse the selection in other images. Adobe Photoshop also lets you go in the other direction—that is, you can save a selection as a path.

For the final image, you want to create type that will wrap around the bottom of the plate. You do this by saving the plate selection as a path and then exporting the path to Adobe Illustrator where you add the curved type.

To turn the selection into a path:

1 Load the Plate selection.

2 Choose Make Path from the Paths palette pop-up menu.

You must convert the selection to a path in order to use it in Adobe Illustrator.

3 Set the Tolerance to 2 and click OK to make the path.

It takes Adobe Photoshop a few seconds to convert the selection into a path.

4 Save the path and name it *Plate Shape.*

5 Save the file.

6 Choose Export from the File menu and Paths from the submenu.

Make sure the Path file name appears as follows:

PHOTOSHP\PHSCIB\PROJECTS\CPOST2.EPS

7 Click OK.

ADDING THE TYPE IN ADOBE ILLUSTRATOR

As in Lesson 12, you can skip this section if you do not have Adobe Illustrator. The DATE.EPS file in the LESSON13 directory contains the type you need to complete this project. To continue creating the poster using the supplied file, turn to the *Placing the Type* section later in this lesson.

If you want more practice in creating type using paths, go ahead and complete this section. If you need help, refer to the detailed instructions for creating type in Adobe Illustrator in Lesson 12.

Entering the type in Adobe Illustrator

The first step toward creating the type is to display the path and enter the text.

To type the date:

1 Open the CPOST2.EPS file in Adobe Illustrator.

2 Click the path-type tool, then click the bottom center of the path to display the insertion point.

3 Type 1990 followed by five spaces, then type 1995.

The type will follow the curve of the path but will be upside down. You'll fix the type in a second.

4 Choose Alignment from the Type menu and Centered from the submenu.

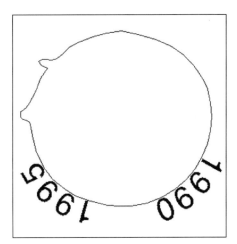

Changing the type style

Now you need to change the font, size, and position of the type.

To change the type style and position:

1 Select all the type.

2 Choose Type Style from the Type menu and click the Fonts button.

3 Select Times Italic and click OK.

4 Enter 36 for Size and click OK.

5 Choose Tracking/Kerning from the Type menu and enter –35 and click OK.

Entering a negative value for Baseline Shift makes the type appear under the path. In this case, the type jumps to the inside of the path.

6 Click the selection tool and drag the top end of the insertion point down, until the type flips beneath the plate.

Filling the type

Right now the type is filled with black. In your Adobe Photoshop poster, the 1995 section of the type appears over a black background. Before bringing the type into the CPOST2.PSD file, you must fill the type with white so it will be visible.

To fill the type:

1 Use the type tool to select the *1995* type.

2 Choose Paint Style from the Paint menu and click White under Fill and click OK.

3 Save the file as DATE1.EPS using the Color Preview option and leave Compatibility set to the default.

4 Exit Adobe Illustrator and return to the CPOST2.PSD file in Adobe Photoshop.

PLACING THE TYPE

You're just about finished with the poster. Your final step is to place the EPS art from the Adobe Illustrator file into the Adobe Photoshop file.

To place the type:

1 With the CPOST2.PSD file active, choose Place from the File menu and open the DATE.EPS file in the LESSON13 directory (or the DATE1.EPS file in the Projects directory if you created it).

2 Click with the gavel to confirm the placement.

It's okay if the date is not in its exact final position. Since the type is a floating selection, you can change the location using the Adobe Photoshop commands.

3 If necessary, use the arrow keys to slightly adjust the type position. The *1* in *1995* should be at about 2-1/2 inches from the left edge of the window.

4 Choose Rotate from the Image menu and Free from the submenu.

5 Rotate the selection until the measurement at the bottom of the Info palette reads from about 3 to 5 degrees.

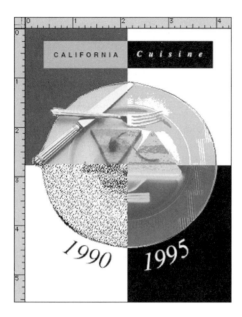

The date should be about one-eighth of an inch below the plate. Use the final image as a reference.

6 Save the file.

CREATING A TWO-TONED DASH

Your poster is just about ready for the trade show. As a finishing touch, you're going to add a dash between the two years.

To create the dash:

1 Create a fixed rectangular marquee that is 20 pixels wide and 5 pixels high.

2 Center the marquee between the two dates (use the division between the black and white background rectangles as a guide).

3 Invert the selection.

This turns the half of the selection in the white rectangle black, and the half of the selection in the black rectangle white.

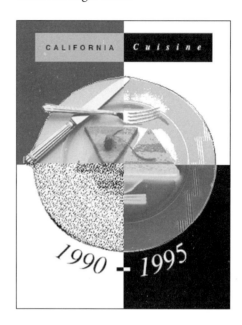

4 Deselect the type and save the file as CPOST3.PSD.

CHANGING THE PRINTING INKS SETUP OPTIONS

As the last procedure in *Classroom in a Book*, you will prepare this image for color separation and print the image.

Before separating the image, you need to check the Printing Inks Setup options and note the dot-gain settings. This example assumes you are printing to a QMS ColorScript printer.

To check the printing setup options:

1 Choose Preferences from the File menu and Printing Inks Setup from the submenu. Notice that when the default SWOP ink is chosen, the dot gain is 20 percent.

2 Close the dialog box and use the eyedropper to sample the blue rectangle in the image.

The Info palette shows the values for this color as about 95 percent cyan, 85 percent magenta, and 0 percent yellow and black.

3 Open the Printing Inks Setup dialog box again and choose QMS ColorScript from the Inks menu.

The default dot gain changes to 25 percent. Remember, dot gain is a method of compensating for different ink coverages. Changing the ink type may require more or less ink to ensure correct color in the final proof.

4 Use the eyedropper to check the blue color values again.

Now the cyan value is 88 percent and the magenta value is 75 percent. This change in values subtracts from the percentage of each plate to compensate for heavier ink coverage on-press.

5 Save the RGB image as CPOST3R.PSD in the Projects directory.

6 Convert the image to CMYK.

PRINTING THE FILE

You can print this file in a number of ways, depending on what you want to see and the type of printer you have available. Although the effect is more dramatic on a color print, you can also try out this printing procedure on a black-and-white printer.

Because this image has white areas that would bleed into a white piece of paper, you're going to add a border as your print. Please make sure you are properly connected to your printer.

To print a composite of the CMYK image:

1 Choose Page Setup from the File menu and click Border.

2 Enter a value of 3 points in the Border dialog box and click OK twice.

3 Choose Print from the File menu and click OK.

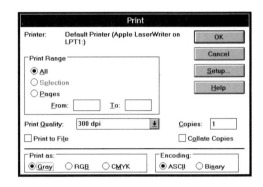

To print color separations of the image:

1 Choose Print from the File menu.

2 Select the Print Separations option and click OK.

The four color plates are printed.

Congratulations! This ends the *Classroom in a Book* lessons. You've accomplished quite a bit since you started just a few days ago with the simple task of making a selection! As you continue to work with Adobe Photoshop, you might want to refer to specific lessons in this book to remind yourself of particular procedures, or remember how to create an individual effect.

For more practice, take the tutorial that comes with your Adobe Photoshop package. As your knowledge and experience expand, you'll probably find the *Adobe Photoshop User Guide* a helpful and comprehensive reference to all of Adobe Photoshop's features and capabilities. Have fun and be creative, as you explore the ever-increasing world of digital imaging.

INDEX

Colophon

DOCUMENTATION

Writing: Kate O'Day, Judith Walthers von Alten, Kisa Harris

Editing: Bob Rumsby, Pat Cook, Susan Clem

Illustrations: Jonathon Caponi, Laura Dower, Andrew Faulkner, Heather Hermstad, Kim Isola

Photographs: Robert Cardellino (Chef, Velvet Curtain), Matthew Farruggio (Crawdads, Wine Glass), Michael LaMotte (Asparagus, Assorted Vegetables, California Cuisine), Scott Peterson (Crab), Charles West (Pasta Factory)

Art direction: Sharon Anderson

Book production: Heather Hermstad, Dawn Dombrow

Book production management: Eve Lynes, Deborah Sparck

Publication management: Joan Delfino

Cover design: Sharon Anderson

Adobe Press: Patrick Ames, Mike Rose

Training Manager: Kisa Harris

Special thanks to: Adobe Technical Support Staff, Carita Klevickis, Mary Anne Petrillo, Nora Sandoval

PRODUCTION NOTES

This book was created electronically using Frame-Maker on the Macintosh, NeXT, and SUN Microsystems Sparc Station IPX workstation. Art was produced using Adobe Illustrator and Adobe Photoshop on the Macintosh and the Windows platform. SnapJot on the Macintosh and Tiffany on the Windows platform were used to capture screen shots. Working film was produced with the PostScript language on a Compugraphic 9600 Imagesetter. The Frutiger and Minion families of typefaces are used throughout this book.

Adobe Training Resources

The Classroom in a Book™ series of training workbooks guides you through step-by-step lessons to help you learn how to master the many powerful features of Adobe Photoshop.

If finding time to focus is difficult, or if you think an instructor-led training program will augment your learning curve, consider investigating some of the many professional training businesses and educational institutions using this very same Classroom in a Book in their classes. Instructors can provide feedback and guidance that go beyond the contents of this book and CD in a classroom setting.

For suggestions, and the name of a licensed Adobe training resource nearest you: In North America, call **Adobe's Customer Services at 1-800-833-6687.** In Europe and the Pacific Rim, call your local distributor.